Pyramid Ascendants

Your Blueprint to Network Marketing Success

Empower Your Entrepreneurial Spirit:

Uncover the Steps to Financial Freedom in Twelve Months, Rise Above the Myths and Build a Successful Network Marketing Business

DUSTIN COHEN, J.D.

DEDICATED TO:

FRANK J. KEEFER

IZHAK BEN SHABAT

JESSE MACPHERSON

Thank you for two decades of friendship, mentorship, and servant leadership. Without each of you I would not have achieved what I have and would not be where I am today!

Dustin Cohen

Preface

"The man who moves a mountain begins by carrying away small stones." — Confucius

In the journey of a thousand miles toward financial independence and entrepreneurial achievement, **network marketing (a.k.a. multi-level marketing, direct sales)** stands as a path not fully understood by many. It is a domain ripe with opportunity but often tarnished by misconception and skepticism.

I've written this book to serve as your compass through the nuanced landscape of network marketing, guiding you from skepticism to mastery, debunking myths, and laying out a concrete map for building a thriving business that brings both financial freedom and personal fulfillment within twelve months.

My motivation for penning this guide stems from a deeply rooted belief in the transformative power of understanding and leveraging the potential of our minds in harmony with steadfast action. My journey through the realms of business entrepreneurship, law, and leading sales teams in high-performing network marketing organizations has crystalized in me the conviction that achieving our loftiest goals is not only possible but inevitable when approached with the right mindset, strategies, and persistence.

I have witnessed firsthand the disillusionment of bright individuals, much like yourselves, who, despite their zeal and hard work, found themselves ensnared in the common pitfalls of network marketing. Their stories of struggle, coupled with the absence of a genuine navigational tool in the industry, propelled me to crystallize my two decades of field experience and insights into this blueprint.

In doing so, I have drawn from a reservoir of knowledge steeped in psychology, business development, and the personal stories of those who have walked the path before – both the triumphs and the trials. My aim is to arm you with not only the technical know-how but also the mental fortitude required to excel in the network marketing industry.

To my mentors, peers, and the countless entrepreneurs whose journeys have inspired these pages, your wisdom and courage have been a light guiding my pen.

I extend my deepest gratitude to you, the reader, for embarking on this journey with me. Your decision to engage with this book signals a readiness to transform your life and impact your community positively. This work is intended for those who are considering network marketing as a path to financial independence, seasoned marketers looking to refine their approach, and skeptics seeking clarity about the industry. No prior network marketing experience is required, just an open mind and the willingness to learn and apply the principles herein.

As we navigate these chapters together, remember, success in direct sales, as in life, is not a destination but a journey of continuous growth, learning, and contribution. **Your potential is limitless**, and within you lies the ability to mold your future into whatever shape you desire.

Thank you for investing your time and trust in this guide. I invite you to continue reading, engage with the concepts, and take the steps laid out in these pages. Your path to **network marketing success** and the prosperous business you dream of is just ahead. Let's begin.

Chapter 1: Igniting the Networking Spark

Jonathan Silverberg stood in the linoleum-tiled kitchen, his forearm resting on the cool granite countertop, thumb pressing against the edge of a frosted glass. The lemonade inside parted around ice cubes like golden islands in a pale sea. A late afternoon sun filtered through the window, laying a honeyed glaze over the quiet suburbia of New Haven. His thoughts traced the bead of condensation dribbling down the side of the glass, meandering to the gathering last night which had flooded him with promises of wealth and growth.

He had always clung to the notion of secure employment, a steady job in a reputable industry. But the invitation from an old college friend, now charismatic as any preacher in the "church" of multi-level marketing (MLM), painted a vivid tableau of dormant potentials waking within him, of connection rich as the purpose they pitched. Jonathan turned towards the small, overgrown garden outside, where a solitary robin scavenged for the evening's fare. Networks of opportunity, they said, branching out like the vines by his window.

The call of his dreams had often been drowned out by pragmatism. Now, as he considered the magnetism of the direct sales company's pitch – the splendor of autonomy, the scaffoldings of self-made success – he found himself at a precipice, one he had edged around his whole career. Could he leap? Communication skills finessed out of necessity; leadership traits forged in the kiln of self-reliance; these were the keystones he could erect his future upon.

He saw his reflection blanched in the stainless-steel fridge, a man on the cusp of transformation or turmoil. A voice within murmured cautions against the capricious winds of fortune that network marketing sailed upon. Yet, a deeper chime resonated with the yearning for recognition, for prosperity interlaced with personal development. He recalled the vibrant testimonials from last night, people who he once knew, now seemingly alight with the flames of their newfound paths – were they kindled by truth or just carefully placed mirrors?

A sudden gust swept through the window, nudging him from his reverie, carrying with it the scent of neighboring barbecues and the distant laughter of children in twilight play. Jonathan wondered where the scales of his ambition and doubt would balance out. Could the personal and professional aspirations he held close marry in the house of a scheme that promised so much yet demanded unfaltering faith? Was he willing to trade the well-trodden path for a gamble upon the stars?

Unleashing the Power of Personal Enterprise

Network marketing represents more than just an opportunity for financial gain - it is a gateway to personal transformation and professional mastery. For those poised on the edge of entrepreneurial endeavor this industry ignites a journey that not only promises income but also a chance to sculpt one's character and skill set. The foundational promise of network marketing is the ability to cultivate a business that thrives on the combined triumphs of its team members, ensuring that your success contributes to the collective prosperity.

Embarking on the quest to build a direct sales business can appear daunting. However, **understanding the underlying principles** is key to unlocking its potential. This early stage is critical, as it sets the tone for your advancement through the tiers of multi-level marketing mastery. By diving into the myriad income streams offered, individuals carve out pathways toward not just financial freedom, but also **personal growth** that transcends the boundaries of conventional employment.

Foster Skills for a Lifetime of Ascendancy

A direct sales business model inherently accentuates the importance of **networking, communication, and leadership**—facets of professional life that many strive to enhance. These are not mere byproducts of a network marketing career; they are the cornerstones upon which your business is built. By fostering these skills deliberately, individuals excel not only within the framework of network marketing but in any collaborative business environment. This chapter aims to elucidate how these skills, once honed, can open doors to opportunities that might have seemed unreachable before.

Your aspirations, both personal and professional, serve as the compass that directs your business trajectory. The beauty of network marketing lies in its flexibility, allowing you to align your business activities with your **ultimate life goals**. This alignment is not serendipitous but the result of meticulous planning and self-analysis. Evaluating these aspirations against the backdrop of direct sales business opportunities, therefore, is not just prudent - it's imperative for anyone serious about making the most of a company's marketing and compensation model.

Realizing Aspirations Through Structured Effort

The roadmap to success is not paved with chance encounters but with structured, strategic efforts. Throughout this guide, we'll explore how to launch and grow a thriving enterprise within this distinctive business structure. You'll be equipped with actionable strategies designed to facilitate a steady march toward your financial and personal objectives, with an emphasis on overcoming the common setbacks that hinder many.

Delving into this system, **patience, persistence, and perseverance** emerge as the virtues that will carry you through. You will learn the art of setting realistic milestones and the importance of celebrating each small victory on your way to the zenith of network marketing success. The concept of sustainable momentum - a continuous drive towards your targets - is not just a hopeful theory but a key ingredient of the blueprint laid out within these pages.

By engaging with this discourse, you step into a community that values **enhancement and contribution**. Here, personal gains are admired, but they resonate even more profoundly when they uplift others in a chain reaction of success and empowerment. This journey, therefore, is not a solitary one; it's a voyage that calls upon your communal spirit and willingness to share knowledge just as much as it does your individual ambition.

The Milestones to Mastery

Advancing from an apprentice to a maestro of multi-level marketing, you will encounter lessons that refine your approach to this lucrative paradigm. Each stage is an opportunity not just for profit, but for invaluable introspection and skill refinement. While network marketing's potential is vast, it is grounded in the practicality that comes with well-researched, evidence-based approaches to market analysis, personal branding, and team leadership.

In the spirit of this **educational journey**, every instruction, every strategy conveyed is meant to build not just a business, but a legacy of learning that you can carry forward into all aspects of your life. This initial chapter is a beacon, illuminating the path ahead - prepare to navigate through the complexities of direct sales with insight, precision, and unwavering resolve.

This industry offers a unique avenue for individuals to explore both **significant income streams** and **personal growth opportunities**. Beyond the conventional realms of employment, multi-level marketing presents a platform where individuals can **harness their entrepreneurial spirit** while pursuing financial success. Through network marketing, one can potentially earn substantial income while simultaneously investing in personal development. This dual benefit is a key factor that sets network marketing apart from traditional career paths. It opens possibilities for individuals to **break away from linear income** and venture into the realm of **leveraged and residual income**.

Starting your own direct sales business not only presents the prospect of **financial abundance** but also serves as a **catalyst for personal growth**. As individuals navigate the network marketing landscape, they are exposed to a multitude of learning opportunities that extend beyond simple sales tactics. This business model offers individuals a chance to develop **prospecting** skills, **enhance communication** abilities, and **nurture leadership** qualities. These skills are invaluable in various aspects of life, not just in the realm of network marketing. They lay the foundation for success in **entrepreneurship, corporate environments**, and even in personal relationships.

By delving into this lucrative industry, individuals can forge connections that extend far beyond mere financial transactions. The networks built within your direct sales company will often prove to be extremely **supportive communities** where team members uplift and assist one another on their paths to success. These networks can provide **mentoring, encouragement**, and a sense of belonging that are crucial elements in personal development. As individuals contribute to the growth of their network, they also experience personal transformation as they learn to **lead, mentor**, and **support** others.

Moreover, network marketing paves the way for individuals to **chart their own course** towards success. Unlike traditional jobs where promotions are often limited by organizational structures, direct sales offer a platform where **progress** is dictated by **effort** and **dedication**. This autonomy empowers individuals to take control of their financial destinies and work towards their desired level of **income** and **achievement**. It is a realm where one's **ambition, drive**, and **skills** directly correlate with the **rewards** reaped.

In essence, network marketing serves as a fertile ground for personal and financial enrichment. It provides individuals with the opportunity to not only **earn a living** but to **craft a lifestyle** aligned with their goals and aspirations. By immersing oneself in the multi-level world, individuals can **unleash their potential**, **cultivate new skills**, and **forge meaningful connections** that propel them towards **achieving personal and financial success** simultaneously.

<u>Continue reading to explore how network marketing can enhance your skills in networking, communication, and leadership.</u>

Multi-level marketing presents an exceptional opportunity for individuals to enhance various skills vital for personal and professional growth. One of the core skills that entrepreneurs can significantly enhance is that of **networking**. While building a direct sales business individuals are encouraged to expand their network and cultivate relationships with a diverse group of people. This process not only helps in expanding one's business reach but also cultivates the ability to establish meaningful connections both within and outside the network marketing framework. Networking within entrepreneurial circles can lead to valuable partnerships, collaborations, and mentorship opportunities, fostering growth both in business acumen and personal relationships.

Another critical skill sharpened through network marketing is **communication**. Effective communication is a cornerstone of success in any endeavor, and network marketing provides a rich platform to practice and refine this skill. Engaging with potential clients, team members, and leaders necessitates clear and concise communication. Moreover, conveying the benefits of products or services persuasively is a skill that is honed within the direct sales industry. From crafting compelling pitches to actively listening to others' needs, network marketing business owners develop a robust communication toolkit that can be applied in various aspects of life.

Leadership is yet another skill that individuals can develop significantly while building your direct sales business. Leading a team within a network marketing organization involves guiding, motivating, and empowering others towards a common goal. Network marketing company entrepreneurs can learn how to inspire and influence others positively, delegate tasks effectively, and provide constructive feedback. These leadership qualities can not only contribute to success within the business but also have a spill-over effect into other areas of life, such as professional endeavors and community involvement.

In essence, network marketing offers a unique platform for individuals to cultivate essential skills that are integral to personal and professional growth. The networking, communication, and leadership abilities honed within the companies training framework not only contribute to success within the business model but also equip individuals with invaluable tools that can be leveraged in various facets of life. By actively engaging in building a direct sales business, individuals can experience tangible growth in these areas, empowering themselves to achieve both financial success and personal development simultaneously.

Aligning Direct Sales Opportunities with Personal Goals

Every individual stepping into the network marketing industry carries a unique set of aspirations. Whether you're seeking financial independence, the flexibility to control your own schedule, or the opportunity to make a tangible difference in the lives of others, this industry can be the vehicle that propels you toward these goals. The key lies in aligning the business model with your personal and professional objectives. To start, create a clear vision of what you wish to achieve. *Are you aiming for short-term gains or long-term wealth creation?* Is professional growth in leadership or sales a priority? Knowing the answers to these questions will guide your decisions as you navigate through the myriad of business venture possibilities.

Crafting a Strategy for Success

Successful network marketing entrepreneurs often treat their business as they would a traditional brick and mortar business - by devising a strategic action plan. Such a plan should include setting realistic income targets, defining timelines, and identifying the skills you need to develop. It is essential to assess whether the products or services offered align with your own values and if the company culture mirrors your own ethos. A thoughtful strategy acts as a roadmap, directing your efforts efficiently and ensuring that every action is a step toward your ultimate objective.

Remember, success in any business is not merely about making sales; it's about developing a sustainable business that grows with you.

The Ripple Effect of Personal Development

Starting a direct sales business isn't just about financial gain; it's a platform for personal development. Network marketing allows you to step out of your comfort zone, enhancing skills that are transferable to other areas of life. For instance, mastering the art of communication in network marketing can lead to stronger relationships and increased confidence in various social situations. The leadership qualities that emerge from building and inspiring a team can elevate your professional prowess beyond the business model's sphere. Your growth within this industry extends a ripple effect, touching upon all facets of your life.

Balancing Act: Personal and Business Life

For many, the allure of network marketing is the promise of a better work-life balance. This business model offers the autonomy to dictate your work hours and the location from which you operate. However, achieving this balance requires discipline. It is crucial to set boundaries to ensure that your business activities enhance rather than encroach upon your personal life. Successful network marketers often segment their day to prioritize tasks and incorporate time for self-care and family, illustrating that striking a balance is not only possible but pivotal to your success.

Leveraging Networks Beyond Sales

Building a downline (direct sales team) within your network marketing business is often misunderstood as merely recruiting to meet sales objectives. In practice, it's about fostering connections and building a community that shares knowledge, support, and opportunities. By investing in these relationships, you don't just expand your business; you enrich your social capital. This cultivates a sense of belonging and can provide insights and assistance in other business ventures, or community projects. In this light, your network becomes a valuable life asset, not just a sales strategy.

Learning from Setbacks

Embracing network marketing means accepting that setbacks and challenges are part of the journey. Each obstacle is an opportunity for learning and growth. Instead of seeing a failed sales pitch or a missed target as a defeat, view it as a lesson in resilience and adaptability. Reflect on what didn't work, adjust your approach, and move forward with newfound wisdom. This iterative process not only furthers your network marketing business but also strengthens your problem-solving skills in all areas of life.

Continuous Education and Adaptation

The landscape of the direct sales industry is dynamic, with trends and tactics constantly evolving. Keeping abreast of industry changes and continuing your education within the field are paramount. Attend workshops, webinars, and conferences to stay informed. Engage with mentors and peers who can provide insights and new perspectives. By remaining adaptable and thirsty for knowledge, you ensure that your business and personal skill set remain relevant and robust.

In essence, evaluating your aspirations and how network marketing aligns with them is foundational to your success in the industry. Approach your business as a comprehensive lifestyle choice, one that affords financial prosperity, personal fulfillment, and unparalleled professional growth. By doing so, you transform the potential of network marketing into your personalized blueprint for achievement.

In the journey ahead, a world of possibilities awaits those who are ready to embrace the power of network marketing. By delving into the realm of multi-level marketing, you are not only unlocking the potential for significant income streams but also opening doors to personal growth and development like never before. **Through direct sales, you can build a thriving team, refine your communication skills, and step into leadership roles that will propel you towards your dreams with unmatched momentum.** The path you are about to embark on is one that promises rewards beyond just financial gain; it is a pathway to becoming the master of your destiny, achieving your aspirations, and soaring to new heights of success. As you turn the pages of this book, get ready to uncover the blueprint that will lead you towards financial freedom in just twelve months. Get set to rise above the myths surrounding the industry and arm yourself with the knowledge and strategies necessary to develop a prosperous direct sales business that reflects your inner drive and entrepreneurial spirit. Embrace the journey ahead, for within these pages lie the keys to unlocking your full potential in the realm of multi-level marketing.

Chapter 2: Work Ethic...More Than Just Dreams

The sun spilled its golden light onto the streets of the small town, where every brick and blade of grass whispered tales of dreams both nurtured and dulled. In one of the modest homes lining the suburban oasis, Mark stood in the silence of his kitchen, gazing through the window which framed his overgrown backyard. His eyes, scanning the relentless wilderness beyond the glass, were pools of reservation. He was not merely looking at the chaotic garden; he saw the reflection of his own journey in multi-level marketing - a path overgrown with the weeds of skepticism and the hardy perennials of hope.

His hands, pressed against the cold granite of the countertop, held steady as he leaned in - a ship's captain braving a brewing storm of doubt. Mark had been told, and had often repeated to himself, the age-old adage that defined success in network marketing as a rarefied echelon, accessible only to those with the right contacts or uncanny charisma. Yet, somewhere deep within him, embers of rebellion glowed. Could not willpower and effort carve a path to prosperity?

Recollections flickered through his mind: late nights spent poring over strategies that promised to elevate, friends who had drifted into memory, their own ventures shipwrecked by false promises. His breaths came slow and deep as he relived each disappointment - each moment a strike of the blacksmith's hammer, hardening the steel of his resolve.

Just as the sun traversed the sky, unnoticed in his reverie, Mark's thoughts wandered to the tales heralded in "Pyramid Ascendants"; accounts of ordinary individuals who, with dogged determination, constructed their success story one day at a time. They had sown their seeds with precision, watered them with diligence, and kept the pests of negativity at bay. Their hands, much like his own now, must have been callused by the toils of their labor—the unseen groundwork of a prosperous network marketing business.

The afternoon waned, pulling Mark back from his musing. He watched children returning from school, their laughter puncturing the still air. They represented a simple truth: perseverance was a lesson well learned in youth, yet its importance never waned. Mark summoned the strength from their carefree spirits, reminded that the willingness to learn and the fervor to persist was a mosaic that anyone could piece together, he included.

The day edged toward twilight, and the play of light and shadow on his face mirrored his internal ruminations. How many sunsets had he seen, each one an echo of the day's labors, a canvas displaying the portrait of time spent in pursuit of an often-misunderstood triumph? He pondered if tomorrow's sunset would find him closer to the vision, he held dear.

As Mark stood there, the quiet sentinel of his own ambition, one cannot help but wonder, what sparks might ignite when belief challenges the notion of the impossible?

Your Career is in Your Hands

The narrative that only a chosen few can excel in multi-level marketing is pervasive and misleading. It is a myth that this chapter seeks to definitively put aside. Network marketing success is not a closed club, reserved for a fortunate select. Rather, success is the product of tireless work ethic, unwavering commitment, and meticulous planning—accessible to anyone. Reaching the pinnacle in network marketing is less about chance and more about choice: the choice to dedicate oneself wholly to the growth of one's business.

The theory that MLM's are inherently unfair, that only early entrants can thrive, is both harmful and incorrect. The reality is that through **robust strategies and consistent efforts**, the playing field levels out. Every entrepreneur in this space can cultivate a **flourishing business**. This chapter explores this reality, dissecting the formula that converts effort into success. It isn't simply about logging hours, but about strategic, intelligent work that aligns with the core principles of network marketing.

Pathways to Prosperity are Paved with Perseverance

An essential aspect to underscore is that dedication is multifaceted. It entails not simply the quantity but the quality of work - laying a **foundation of strategic action**. One must balance patience with persistence, learning the ropes while seizing opportunities. To this end, the chapter introduces practical tools and anecdotes - all curated to guide and inspire. These resources serve as a testament to the power of diligence and strategic planning in the journey toward network marketing mastery.

Empowerment in network marketing comes from understanding that **hard work is a variable that you can control**. Unlike external factors that may ebb and flow, your commitment to the grind is a constant. It's this realization that transforms a dreamer into a doer - and your network marketing business from a fledgling endeavor into a lucrative enterprise. This shift in mindset and consequent action is critical for anyone aspiring to rise within the network marketing ranks.

Unlock the Lessons of Endurance

Moreover, the chapter delves into the essence of perseverance, a trait often overshadowed by the flashy allure of quick success. In network marketing, as in any business, the willingness to endure, to adapt and to **continuously learn**, can make all the difference. It is the sustained effort over time, coupled with the readiness to evolve, that builds a resilient business capable of weathering the unpredictable storms of the marketplace.

Understanding the nature of the network marketing business landscape is akin to learning a new language; *mastery comes with time and practice.* Here, readers will find guidance to navigate the intricacies of this business model, fostering skills and strategies necessary for growth. The discussion navigates the challenging terrains of network marketing, providing insights that are not only theoretical but also *practically applicable* in the real-world scenarios of networking and sales.

Cultivate Your Craft with Confidence

Confidence in your decision to build a network marketing business derives from acknowledging and harnessing your individual power to effect change. This chapter serves as a *mentor's nudge*, steering away from complacency and towards proactive advancement. It supports a mission to elevate your business acumen and refine the skills essential to thrive in the business.

In stitching together these key lessons, the narrative reiterates a poignant truth: success is not bestowed, it is built. Through the synthesis of potent anecdotes and authoritative guidance, this chapter stands as a blueprint for action - a catalyst for transformation in both professional mindset and method. It lays bare the blueprint for success in network marketing, reinforcing that with the right approach, success isn't only possible - it's probable.

Success in this industry is not reserved for a select few, as commonly believed. **The myth of exclusivity perpetuates the idea that only a chosen elite can thrive in the world of multi-level marketing.** This misconception often deters individuals from exploring the opportunities that network marketing can offer. It is essential to debunk this myth and clarify that success in network marketing is accessible to anyone who is willing to put in the effort. By dispelling the notion of an exclusive club, aspiring entrepreneurs can shift their mindset towards a more achievable goal.

Contrary to popular belief, network marketing success is not about luck or privilege; it is about dedication and hard work. Those who excel in this field do so through persistent effort and strategic planning. By understanding the importance of commitment and strong work ethic, individuals pave their way towards financial prosperity from their network marketing business. It is crucial to recognize that success does not come overnight; it requires consistent effort and a willingness to learn and adapt.

Accessibility to success in network marketing is not limited by background, education, or previous experience. While these factors may influence the journey, they do not determine the ultimate outcome. With the right mindset and a willingness to learn and grow, anyone can succeed in a network marketing business. It is essential to shift focus from perceived barriers to opportunities for growth and development.

By embracing the idea that network marketing success is within reach for all who are dedicated, individuals can unlock their true potential. This shift in perspective empowers aspiring entrepreneurs to take ownership of their journey and strive for excellence. Through practical tools and guidance, individuals can navigate the complexities of the multi-level marketing world with confidence and determination.

Dismantling the myth of exclusivity opens a world of possibilities for those willing to pursue success in network marketing. By understanding that hard work, dedication, and strategic action are the keys to building a prosperous business, individuals can set themselves on a path towards achievement. The journey to network marketing success is not limited to a select few; it is an open road waiting to be traveled by those with the drive and determination to succeed.

Read on to discover how embracing hard work, dedication, and strategic planning can propel you towards success in the dynamic world of network marketing.

Success in the world of network marketing is not just about dreaming big; it's about putting in the hard work, dedication, and strategic actions necessary to build a thriving business. Embracing these key elements is crucial in creating a prosperous network marketing venture that can withstand the challenges and uncertainties of the industry.

Hard work is the backbone of success in direct sales. It involves dedicating time and effort consistently to grow your business, reach out to potential customers, and build a strong network of distributors. Without a strong work ethic, even the most brilliant ideas and strategies can fall short.

Dedication is another essential component in the network marketing journey. It requires staying committed to your goals, even when faced with obstacles or setbacks. Dedication means showing up every day, putting in the effort to learn and improve, and persisting through challenges. In the competitive landscape of network marketing, dedication sets successful entrepreneurs apart from those who give up at the first sign of difficulty. It is the drive that fuels progress and propels individuals towards their desired outcomes.

Strategic action is the deliberate planning and implementation of steps to achieve specific objectives in your business. It involves setting goals, creating a roadmap to reach them, and making calculated decisions to move closer to success.

Strategic action requires foresight, adaptability, and a willingness to learn from both successes and failures. By approaching their business strategically, individuals can optimize their efforts, maximize their resources, and stay ahead of the curve in a dynamic market environment.

In this industry, success is not guaranteed solely by luck or chance; it is earned through a combination of hard work, dedication, and strategic acumen. Those who excel in network marketing understand that building a prosperous business requires a proactive approach, continuous learning, and a willingness to evolve with the industry's demands. By embracing the core values of hard work, dedication, and strategic action, individuals can unlock their full potential and achieve remarkable results in the industry.

Success in network marketing is not reserved for a select few; it is within reach for anyone willing to put in the effort. By embracing the ethos of hard work, dedication, and strategic thinking, individuals can carve out a successful path in the industry. Each step taken with purpose and determination brings them closer to their goals and reinforces the belief that success in network marketing is attainable with the right mindset and actions.

Recognizing the Role of Perseverance

The landscape of multi-level marketing is such that it calls not just for a visionary's dream but a worker's grit. Thriving in a network marketing business demands an indomitable spirit of perseverance. It's the sustained effort after initial enthusiasm has waned and when the challenges begin to pile up. This perseverance becomes the bridge between early failures and later successes.

The reality of network marketing, much like any other entrepreneurial venture, is punctuated by obstacles and setbacks. But it is the tenacious pursuit of one's goals that differentiates successful participants from those who falter. **Consistently pushing your limits** and embracing the grind will eventually refine your strategy and amplify your outcomes.

The Willingness to Learn is Paramount

True network marketing mastery lies in an unyielding willingness to learn. This industry continues to evolve, and so should the network marketing professional. **Knowledge is a currency** and ongoing education is your investment in the ever-changing market of network marketing. Embrace every training session, webinar, and conference not just as a formality, but as a critical opportunity to absorb new tactics and insights. The willingness to learn also encompasses learning from your network - listening to customer feedback, observing your mentors, and collaborating with peers. Such an approach infuses your business model with fresh perspectives and keeps you ahead of the curve.

Leveraging Setbacks as Learning Opportunities

Setbacks can be disheartening, but they are also replete with insights. Instead of viewing them as failures, reframe these experiences as constructive feedback. This is the fabled 'learning from your mistakes' in action. When a strategy does not yield the expected results, dissect it to understand why. This practice of critical self-evaluation and adapting is a hallmark of a growth mindset. It's crucial to not only bounce back from setbacks but to emerge stronger, with improved strategies and renewed vigor. *Transform each of these moments into steppingstones* that lead you closer to your network marketing goals.

Cultivating Patience in Your Network Marketing Journey

The fruits of labor in network marketing do not ripen overnight. Patience is instrumental in allowing your efforts to fully develop their potential. Understand that building a sustainable team and seeing substantial growth takes time. Immediate results might be motivating, but the true measure of success is seen in the sustainability and long-term growth of your business. **Patience is a facilitator of quality**, ensuring that you do not rush decisions or fall for shortcuts that compromise the integrity of your business model.

Building Resilience Against Rejection

Rejection is an inherent aspect of sales-oriented industries, and network marketing is no exception. Developing a resilient mindset is thus vital. It's about not taking rejections personally, but rather analyzing each "no" for any constructive criticism it may contain. Resilience builds character and forges the sort of mental toughness that ensures such refusals do not detract from your business goals. When rejection loses its sting, you gain the freedom to approach prospects with confidence, learning with each interaction to refine your pitch and approach.

The Importance of Setting Realistic Goals

Goal setting is as much about the endgame as it is about setting realistic, incremental targets. These smaller milestones provide clarity and focus, allowing you to track progress and celebrate achievements along the way. They serve to motivate and guide your efforts. Importantly, they must be flexible enough to adapt to changes and challenges in the business environment. Realistic goals are the scaffolding upon which a resilient network marketing strategy is constructed.

Commit to Continual Improvement

Resting on one's laurels is not a luxury granted to those who wish to succeed in network marketing. Embrace the concept of kaizen, or continuous improvement. This Japanese philosophy espouses the practice of perpetually seeking ways to enhance your business operations and personal skills. Keeping up with industry trends, refining your marketing tactics, and enriching your product knowledge are just a few of the avenues through which you can maintain a trajectory of improvement. **Every day offers an opportunity to be better** than you were the day before.

Embracing Change as a Catalyst for Growth

In the dynamic world of direct sales, adaptability is a key characteristic of successful entrepreneurs. Market trends and consumer behaviors are constantly in flux, and your ability to pivot and embrace change can set you apart. Viewing change as a catalyst for growth is instrumental in keeping your business model relevant and responsive. It's not about fearing the new, but about harnessing its potential to bolster and invigorate your enterprise.

Fostering a Community of Shared Knowledge

Finally, recognize the immense value in creating a supportive network where shared knowledge becomes the bedrock of collective success. As you learn and grow, impart that knowledge to others within your network marketing community. By fostering an environment of mutual learning and support, you contribute significantly to a culture of success. *Empowerment through education* is a powerful force that can ripple through your network, elevating not just individual members but the entire group. This collaborative approach helps everyone to rise together, solidifying the foundation for a prosperous business journey.

Success is not reserved for a chosen few but rather for those with the **dedication, hard work, and strategic mindset** to make it happen. By dispelling myths surrounding the exclusivity of success, we pave the way for a new understanding: it is within the grasp of anyone willing to put in the effort.

Embrace the sweat equity required to build a thriving network marketing business. It's not just about dreams; it's about concrete actions and unwavering commitment. Make every task, no matter how small, a steppingstone toward your goals. With each dedicated effort, you are shaping your path to success.

Perseverance is the cornerstone of achievement in the network marketing world. Stay committed when faced with challenges, setbacks, or naysayers. Your resolve to continue learning, adapting, and growing is what sets you apart on the journey towards financial independence.

Recognize that **success in network marketing** is not a lottery win but a result of continuous learning and relentless effort. Stay vigilant and open-minded, always seeking new knowledge and innovative strategies to propel your business forward. As you cultivate these qualities, you not only elevate your chances of success but also inspire others to follow in your determined footsteps.

Chapter 3: Believing in Your Network Marketing Brand

Jonathan found himself standing in the quiet churn of an early morning coffee shop, the subtle aroma of roasted beans mingling with the whispered chatter of early risers. His reflection on the windowpane stared back at him, a pale ghost superimposed on the awakening street. He cradled a warm cup, the steam rising like a summons to the day's daunting challenge.

He pondered the weight of his responsibility, the web of faces behind each distributor in his network, trust threaded through each interaction, delicate yet tenacious. The business was a ship he aimed to steer with integrity, away from the iceberg of short-term profit and towards the open sea of longevity. He recalled the early days, the allure of quick success, now transmuted into a quest for sustainable growth, a test of ethics more grueling than any he had prepared for.

Conversations swirled around him, transactions of both currency and camaraderie. He observed the natural exchange between mentor and apprentice across the room - a tradesman sharing expertise with eager, unlined faces. Jonathan's thoughts aligned in parallel, considering how his own guidance might shape the destiny of his charges. The art of mentorship, he mused, was less about imparting wisdom and more about fostering discovery, a subtle dance where each step was a lesson in trust.

He sipped his coffee, and warmth bloomed within him, mirroring the warmth he sought to cultivate within his business relationships. Glances from his digital watch to his notebook filled with strategies and reflections were interrupted by the clink of porcelain, the rustle of coats, the ebb and flow of a morning gathering momentum. He knew that transparency was his compass, his decisions a map for others to follow or forsake.

Would the seeds of collaboration blossom into a forest of mutual success, or wither in the barren soil of mistrust? He left the shop, the door swinging close with the tinkle of a bell, the quiet hum of possibility echoing in his mind. He walked on, every stride a testament to his conviction in the power of a business built on ethical bedrock. But the question that now turned over and over in his mind like a leaf caught in a gentle stream was: Can the roots of integrity delve deep enough to weather the storms of an industry rife with skepticism?

The Cornerstone of Credibility in Network Marketing

When it comes to multi-level marketing the difference between ascent and descent lies within the realm of ethical practice and transparency. Establishing a foundation of trust is not merely a moral choice but a strategic imperative for those who aspire to thrive in this challenging and often misunderstood industry.

Ethics serve as the backbone of a sustainable network marketing business, guiding interactions with potential recruits, customers, and fellow network marketers. As you forge ahead in molding your empire, this chapter posits the principles of ethical conduct as non-negotiable pillars supporting your journey towards financial freedom.

Transparency is the currency of trust in an industry where skepticism is the status quo. Grasping this concept is pivotal for business builders who are serious about distinguishing themselves in a competitive marketplace. Adopting transparent business practices is not just about adhering to legal requirements; it involves genuine communication about product efficacy, earnings potential, and business operations.

By embodying these values, entrepreneurs cement their reputation and foster an environment that encourages growth and longevity.

Cultivating a Culture of Collective Success

The art of collaboration in direct sales reflects a tapestry interwoven with the threads of shared success and mutual learning. **Mentorship is not a mere transfer of knowledge but an exchange of value** that strengthens the fabric of the entire network.

Seasoned network marketing leaders know the significance of nurturing relationships based on respect, equity, and the shared goal of elevating every member of the community. Within these relationships lies the potential for exponential growth, not just of individual businesses but for the entire industry.

As entrepreneurs embrace network marketing's legitimacy, they'll begin fostering a strong community of likeminded, success-driven, team members. This undertaking involves more than just personal gain; it's about contributing to a broader business ecosystem that thrives on supportive connections. By investing time and resources into helping others succeed, you effectively build a resilient network that acts as a safety net during challenging times. A community spirit underscored by ethical practices not only propels your business forward but also creates a ripple effect, elevating the industry standard.

Integrity: Your Network Marketing Business Lifeline

The quest for longevity in this industry demands a steadfast commitment to integrity. It requires a long-term vision that prioritizes sustainable growth over quick fixes and fleeting successes. Integrity is the crucible within which your business's reputation is forged. A resolute adherence to ethical standards will differentiate your venture as one that is reliable and grounded in principled actions. In this chapter, you will explore actionable ways to maintain the integrity of your business while ensuring its long-term viability.

Navigating the business landscape with ethical clarity is paramount. As you implement the strategies discussed herein, reflect on how each decision aligns with your core values and the overarching goal of creating a prosperous business. Remember, success in network marketing is not an individual sport; it's a collective endeavor that blossoms in the presence of transparency, camaraderie, and unyielding ethical commitment.

The journey of mastering the multi-level marketing industry is paved with challenges, but bearing the torch of ethics will illuminate your path towards enduring success. Take this chapter as your roadmap to infusing your business practices with integrity, fostering collaborative growth, and ultimately achieving a resilient and rewarding career. By harnessing the principles outlined here, you are not simply climbing the ladder of success; you are ensuring each rung is securely fastened with the unbreakable strength of your ethical convictions.

In the world of direct sales the importance of ethical practices and transparency cannot be overstated. These pillars serve as the foundation for trust, credibility, and long-term success within the industry. Building a sustainable business requires a commitment to honesty, integrity, and a genuine belief in the products or services you are promoting. When you operate ethically and transparently, you not only cultivate a loyal customer base but also gain the respect of your peers and competitors. **By upholding high ethical standards, you differentiate yourself from less reputable individuals in the industry, setting yourself up for long-lasting success.**

Ethical practices in network marketing involve more than just following the rules and regulations set forth by governing bodies. It means **conducting business with honesty, fairness, and a genuine desire to help others achieve their goals**.

Transparency is equally vital, as it involves being open and honest about your business practices, compensation structure, and product offerings. **When you communicate openly with your downline, customers, and potential recruits, you build trust and credibility, essential components of a thriving network marketing business.**

In an industry often marred by misconceptions and skepticism, ethical behavior stands out as a beacon of authenticity and reliability. **By embodying integrity in all aspects of your network marketing business, you not only attract like-minded individuals but also contribute to the overall positive reputation of the industry.** Your commitment to ethical practices not only benefits your own business but also elevates the community, fostering an environment where trust and collaboration thrive.

As you embark on your entrepreneurial journey, remember that ethical practices and transparency are not just buzzwords; they are the cornerstones of a successful and sustainable business. By placing a strong emphasis on these principles, you not only ensure your own success but also help raise the standards of the entire industry. **Ultimately, building a credible and ethical network marketing business requires a steadfast commitment to doing what is right, even when faced with challenges or temptations.**

Continue reading to discover how fostering a culture of collaboration and mentorship can further enhance your network marketing journey.

Building a successful direct sales business requires fostering a culture of collaboration and learning the art of mentorship to develop trustworthy relationships within the community. **Collaboration** in network marketing involves working together towards common goals, sharing knowledge and resources, and supporting each other's success. By engaging in collaborative efforts, individuals can tap into a collective pool of skills and experiences, enhancing the overall growth and development of the network marketing network.

Mentorship plays a vital role in guiding newcomers and helping them navigate the complexities of the network marketing industry. Establishing mentor-mentee relationships fosters a sense of trust, respect, and accountability within the network. Seasoned network marketing professionals can offer valuable insights, advice, and support to those who are just starting, helping them avoid common pitfalls and accelerate their progress towards success.

Creating a **culture** that values collaboration and mentorship not only benefits individual members but also strengthens the entire network marketing community. By actively participating in mentorship programs, sharing knowledge, and supporting one another's growth, individuals contribute to the overall success and sustainability of the network. This collective effort builds a sense of unity, trust, and camaraderie that are essential for long-term success in network marketing.

Trustworthy relationships are the foundation of a successful network marketing business. By prioritizing ethical practices, transparency, and integrity in all interactions, individuals can build credibility and earn the trust of their peers and customers. Trust is a key component of long-lasting relationships, and it is essential for creating a loyal customer base and a strong network of downline team members.

In network marketing, mentorship goes beyond just providing guidance; it involves **empowering** others to reach their full potential. Effective mentors not only share their knowledge and experience but also inspire and motivate their mentees to set ambitious goals and strive for excellence. By nurturing talent, fostering growth, and celebrating achievements, mentors play a crucial role in developing the next generation of network marketing leaders.

Through collaboration and mentorship, individuals can **leverage** the collective expertise and support of the company's community to overcome challenges, capitalize on opportunities, and achieve sustainable success. By actively engaging in collaborative efforts, seeking out mentorship relationships, and upholding ethical standards, network marketing professionals can cultivate a thriving network built on trust, credibility, and shared values.

In summary, fostering a culture of collaboration, embracing mentorship, and prioritizing trustworthy relationships are essential pillars for building a successful business. By actively engaging with the community, learning from experienced mentors, and upholding ethical practices, individuals can establish a strong foundation for long-term growth and prosperity in the network marketing industry.

Maintaining Integrity and Trustworthiness

As a business professional integrity should be the cornerstone of your business strategy. Upholding high ethical standards is not only about avoiding questionable practices, but it's also about consistently aligning your actions with transparent values. This means being honest with your team, your customers, and yourself about the nature of the products, the sustainability of the business model, and the realistic outcomes of enrollment. **Operate with candor**, and you'll foster a culture where trust blooms—a vital component in the world where word-of-mouth is a currency of its own.

The Ethical Use of Testimonials and Claims

In promoting network marketing products or services, be cautious of the claims made by the company or fellow distributors. Misrepresentation, even when accidental, can have profound legal and reputational consequences. Use testimonials properly—ensure they are genuine, verifiable, and that they do not promise typical results if those results are, in fact, not typical. When discussing earnings and success rates, provide clear disclaimers about the average earnings and highlight the hard work required to achieve success, so as not to mislead prospects.

Sustainability through Customer Focus

Rather than solely recruiting distributors, *concentrate on acquiring and retaining satisfied customers*. A robust customer base is indicative of product value and market demand, confirming the legitimacy and longevity of your business. Embrace customer feedback, addressing concerns and improving service. A thriving customer-centric approach will often naturally generate interest from customers wanting to become distributors, knowing firsthand the value of what they are promoting.

Continuing Education and Compliance

Stay informed about the regulations governing network marketing practices. Attend company-provided training and seek third-party educational resources that help you navigate the legal landscape. Encouraging your team to prioritize compliance and emphasizing its importance can't be overstated - it safeguards your business and can dramatically reduce the risk of infractions that could tarnish your brand's reputation.

Financial Transparency

Be upfront about the financial aspect of your network marketing business. Openly discuss start-up costs, ongoing expenses, and realistic earnings. Help your team understand budget management and the importance of not overspending in pursuit of growth. Providing your network with tools for financial responsibility is a powerful way to demonstrate ethical leadership and protect participants from potential financial strain.

Focusing on Personal Development

Encourage and invest in personal and professional growth—both in yourself and in your distributors. Offer or recommend resources for skills enhancement and leadership development. The growth of a network marketing business is directly tied to the growth of its distribution network. As they become more capable and knowledgeable, they are better equipped to make informed decisions and act with integrity.

Building a Legacy of Positive Impact

Lastly, view your business as an opportunity to leave a positive impact on the lives of your customers and team members. By promoting a product, you believe in and doing so in an ethical and transparent way, you can help uplift the network marketing industry's reputation. *Your legacy will be defined by the influence you had on others*, and the respect and trust you've earned will far outlive immediate financial success, seeding a business that thrives on its integrity.

As you conclude this chapter on ethical practices and transparency within the industry, remember that **integrity is the cornerstone of a successful network marketing business.** Building trust among your team and customers is not just a choice but a necessity for long-term viability. By embracing ethical principles and fostering a culture of collaboration, you lay a solid foundation for your network marketing journey.

Transparency is not just a buzzword; it's a guiding principle that should permeate every aspect of your business. When you operate with openness and honesty, you build credibility and attract those who value integrity in their business dealings.

Mentorship is not just about teaching; it's about nurturing relationships that are built on trust and mutual respect. As you seek guidance from mentors and become a mentor yourself, remember that these connections are invaluable in shaping your entrepreneurial path towards success.

Your commitment to ethical conduct and transparency will set you apart in the competitive world of multi-level marketing. Remember, the path to prosperity is paved with **integrity, collaboration, and a steadfast belief in the ethical foundation of your business.** Stand firm in your values and lead by example as you watch your network marketing business thrive through principled actions.

Chapter 4: Cultivating a Success Focused Mindset

Amidst the hum of a suburban afternoon, sunlight spilled through the open windows of a modest home office where Samantha labored over her business. multi-level marketing - these three words had become both her challenge and her beacon. A cascade of phone calls and messages competed for her attention, but within the bustle lay an undercurrent of uncertainty, a whisper of doubt that she worked to stifle.

She paused, thumb hovering above the glowing screen of her smartphone. A mentor's advice ebbed into her thoughts, suggesting she harness the power of positive psychology to fuel her endeavors. Success was not merely about sales and numbers; it was about crafting an optimistic vision for her future. The idea of being truly attuned with her inner mindset glistened on the horizon of her desires. "Could an unfaltering belief in abundance transform my reality?" she wondered silently.

As afternoon turned to evening, shades of orange and purple painted the sky. The thoughts of past failures and rejections threatened to creep in like shadows with the setting sun, but resilience took hold. Samantha's resolve steeled as she recalled overcoming objections and closed deals that once seemed insurmountable. A smile gradually took residence on her face as she pondered the growth she had witnessed - not just in her business, but within herself. She acknowledged the sting of disappointments, yet they seemed less poignant now, overpowered by the realization that with each setback, her tenacity grew.

In the quiet space between heartbeats, the distant laughter of children playing outside broke her reverie, and Samantha's eyes wandered to a shelf lined with books espousing personal development. The spines, creased with use, held stories and strategies that resonated with her journey. Incorporating these teachings into her daily ritual had become second nature, much like breathing. Each chapter read, each idea implemented, was a step towards an enriched life and a thriving business. Continuous learning had become the bedrock of her growth.

The crust of daily life settled into a comfortable lull as dusk encroached. Samantha's home cooled with the night air. The suburban choir - the rustle of leaves, the creak of trees, the symphony of crickets - played just for her. In this moment, she recognized the intersection of personal growth with business acumen, an intimate dance where one could not flourish without the other. The revelation was as clear as the stars that began to dot the night sky: her success in the multi-level marketing landscape was as much about developing her character as it was about expanding her network.

A deep breath filled her lungs, a reservoir of calmness. Thoughts drifted to the network of individuals under her guidance. How could she instill this same blend of self-growth and business strategy in them? Samantha knew the answer was etched in the example she set, the culture she cultivated. But as the moon climbed higher, casting silvery ripples across the room, the thought lingered: Are the seeds of personal development enough to rise above the labyrinth of multi-level marketing and reach the peak of success?

Mindset Matters: The Invisible Framework for Network Marketing Triumph

When we talk about the sturdy pillars that uphold the towering edifices of multi-level marketing the most robust of them isn't visible to the naked eye. It's the **mindset** that entrepreneurs carry within. This unseen foundation determines whether the structure soars or crumbles under pressure. In network marketing, you quickly realize that your personal development is not just a companion to your business - it **is** your business. The strategies and techniques that fill the pages of guides and seminars are important, but they pale in comparison to the power of a well-cultivated mind.

Understanding the intersection of **positive psychology** and business success is the first step in this cultivation. An entrepreneur must comprehend the science of happiness and motivation to thrive. **Positive psychology** illuminates the path to resilience, showing how optimism fuels progress and how one's attitude towards setbacks can be more important than the setbacks themselves. Mastery in network marketing is predicated not just on products and pitches, but on one's ability to maintain psychological well-being in the face of adversity.

Resilience and Abundance: Your Armor and Ammunition

Business is a battle, and network marketing is no different. To arm oneself adequately, one must build resilience like armor and develop an **abundance mentality** as their weaponry. The journey will be fraught with challenges - rejected invitations, fluctuating income, and skepticism from peers. It is the entrepreneur's resilience that allows them to stand strong, and their belief in abundance that ensures they never see opportunities as scarce. By viewing the world as a reservoir of endless possibility, network marketing professionals can look beyond temporary defeat, see the bigger picture, and strategize for future victories.

Continuous personal development is not an optional add-on; it's the fuel that keeps the network marketing engine running. Learning is a continuous spiral that feeds into itself, with each lesson propelling you upwards. It's about enhancing your skills, staying agile in the face of industry trends, and being ready to pivot when necessary. Integrating continuous learning into your business strategy ensures that growth is not episodic but a sustained upward trajectory.

The Path to Peak Performance

Performance in network marketing is not just measured in sales or ranks achieved; it's gauged by how much you've evolved as a person and a professional. Strategies may shift and products might change, but the personal insights you gain are enduring assets. Embracing the journey of **self-improvement** is embracing a commitment to excellence in all facets of life. It instills a discipline that transcends the immediate boundaries of network marketing, fostering habits and mindsets that will serve you across any business venture, relationship, or personal ambition.

Joining Hands with Positive Psychology

The influence of **positive psychology in network marketing** extends beyond individual success; it radiates outwards, creating a culture of positivity that can transform teams and communities. When leaders operate from a place of psychological strength, they become beacons of inspiration for their downlines. This chain reaction of optimism can elevate an entire team, proving that when you invest in developing the mind, the dividends benefit many.

Launching Your Personal Development Rocket

Taking the initiative in **personal development** requires a willingness to assess oneself honestly, recognize areas for improvement, and take decisive action to address them. It is an invitation to be an eternal student of life, never settling, and confidently stepping into arenas that may once have been intimidating. True network marketing mastery combines sharp business acumen with an unquenchable thirst for self-betterment.

In the direct sales industry, where potentials are abundant, and the only real ceiling is the one we impose on ourselves, embarking on a journey of mindset cultivation is the key to unlocking limitless opportunities. As distributors, entrepreneurs, and visionaries, the greatest service we can render to ourselves and those we influence is to commit to the path of **unyielding personal growth**. We must remember, the seeds of our business are planted in the fertile soil of our minds; nurturing it ensures a harvest that far exceeds our initial imaginings. With each chapter of our development, we not only elevate our business but also contribute to a grander societal well-being. The message is clear: **cultivate your**

mind, nurture your spirit, and watch your network marketing business, and your life, flourish beyond measure.

Positive psychology holds a key role in the success of individuals building a direct sales business. This branch of psychology focuses on harnessing strengths, fostering optimism, and promoting overall well-being. In the context of network marketing, a positive mindset can be the differentiating factor between those who thrive and those who falter. By cultivating a mindset that embraces possibilities, individuals can reshape how they perceive challenges, setbacks, and opportunities within the marketplace.

One crucial aspect of positive psychology in multi-level marketing is the emphasis on self-belief and confidence. **Believing in one's ability to succeed** is a cornerstone of building a sustainable network marketing business. When individuals have a strong sense of self-worth and believe in their capacity to achieve their goals, they exhibit resilience in the face of obstacles. This resilience propels them forward, even in the most turbulent times, leading to long-term business success.

Moreover, positive psychology encourages **gratitude and appreciation** as powerful tools for personal growth. In network marketing, expressing gratitude for successes, no matter how small, can fuel motivation and create a positive feedback loop.

By acknowledging achievements and progress, individuals maintain a sense of momentum and drive that propels their business forward. Gratitude also fosters a sense of fulfillment and contentment, essential elements for long-term success in any endeavor, including network marketing.

An abundant mindset is another critical component of positive psychology in network marketing. **Embracing abundance** means shifting from a scarcity mentality to one of limitless possibilities. When individuals believe in the plethora of opportunities available to them in the network marketing space, they approach challenges with a sense of creativity and resourcefulness. This mindset attracts success and opens doors to new avenues for growth and expansion within the network marketing network.

Diving deeper into the principles of positive psychology and their transformational impact on network marketing success...

In the dynamic world of multi-level marketing challenges can arise that test the mettle of even the most determined entrepreneurs. Developing resilience and fostering an abundance mentality are essential traits that can propel individuals towards success in the face of adversity. **Resilience** is the ability to bounce back from setbacks and failures, learning from them rather than being defeated. It involves maintaining a positive outlook and adapting to changes with grace and determination.

Embracing an abundance mentality requires believing in the limitless possibilities for growth and success, both for oneself and for others. This mindset focuses on collaboration rather than competition, recognizing that there is more than enough room for everyone to thrive in the network marketing field. By cultivating this mindset, individuals can shift their perspective from scarcity to abundance, opening new opportunities for personal and professional development.

Overcoming network marketing challenges requires a combination of resilience, courage, and a willingness to learn from mistakes. Rather than viewing obstacles as insurmountable barriers, successful entrepreneurs see them as opportunities for growth and improvement. By embracing challenges as steppingstones to success, individuals can transform setbacks into launching pads for greater achievements.

To build resilience, one must practice self-care, maintain a positive support system, and continuously engage in personal development activities. By taking care of one's physical, emotional, and mental well-being, individuals can strengthen their ability to face challenges head-on and emerge stronger on the other side. Surrounding oneself with a supportive network of like-minded individuals who uplift and encourage can also provide the necessary foundation for staying resilient in the face of adversity.

Nurturing an abundance mentality involves shifting from a mindset of scarcity to one of abundance. Instead of seeing limitations and constraints, individuals with an abundance mentality see possibilities and opportunities at every turn. This shift in mindset not only unlocks creativity and innovation but also fosters a sense of generosity and collaboration with others in the community.

By developing resilience and an abundance mentality, individuals can navigate the twists and turns of their business with grace and determination. These qualities serve as pillars of strength, enabling entrepreneurs to weather storms, overcome obstacles, and emerge victorious in their pursuit of financial freedom. Through perseverance, optimism, and a commitment to personal growth, those who make the decision to be true professionals can rise above challenges and achieve their long-term business goals.

Embrace Constant Learning as a Core Strategy

In the realm of multi-level marketing, your education never truly ends. Continuous personal development is not an optional extra; it's a fundamental strategy for sustained growth. You must remain a perpetual student of both business and life. This means dedicating time to learn new skills, staying abreast with the latest industry trends, and consistently sharpening your mind. **Invest in books, seminars, and courses** that not only cover network marketing-specific topics but also broader subjects like marketing, psychology, and communication. By doing so, you amplify your capabilities, giving yourself a competitive edge that can translate into tangible business successes.

Set Goals for Personal Growth

Just as you set business objectives, carve out milestones for your own development. What new skill or knowledge do you aim to acquire this quarter? How will it benefit your network marketing endeavors? A regular self-audit holds you accountable and gives direction to your learning. Set specific, measurable, achievable, relevant, and time-bound (SMART) goals that challenge and expand your skill set. Understand that every piece of knowledge assimilated has the potential to **unlock new avenues for income and influence**.

Harness the Power of Mentoring

Mentoring doesn't just occur in formal settings; it's a resource to tap into within your network marketing community. Seek out relationships with network marketing veterans and thought leaders, engaging them as mentors. True wisdom often comes from shared experiences and having a mentor means benefiting from years of successes and mistakes. Establish a mentor-mentee relationship with someone whose achievements and values align with your aspirations. This fast-tracks you're learning and helps you avoid common pitfalls, saving you time and energy.

Inspire Others Through Your Own Development

As you grow, let your journey inspire others. When team members see your commitment to personal development, it motivates them to follow suit. Encourage a *culture of learning* within your network, where everyone is constantly improving and contributing. Share your insights and celebrate the advancement of others. This not only strengthens your team's overall capabilities but creates a supportive environment where **everyone is pushing towards a shared vision**.

Adapt Mindfulness Techniques for Focus and Clarity

Incorporate mindfulness and mental well-being practices into your routine. Network marketing can be fast-paced and stressful, making balance and focus crucial. Techniques such as meditation, journaling, or just regular self-reflection can enhance your mental clarity and decision-making. Clean mental space enables you to **absorb new information effectively** and apply it with precision. Make no mistake - mental stamina is just as important as business knowledge in the pursuit of excellence.

Prioritize Health for Peak Performance

Never underestimate the link between physical health and mental acuity. A healthy diet, regular exercise, and adequate rest are not only good for your personal welfare; they're part of maintaining the high energy levels required for success. When your body is at its peak, so is your ability to learn, engage, and persuade. Approach your health as you would any business asset – **with a strategy to maximize its value**.

Embrace Feedback as a Learning Tool

Feedback is crucial for personal growth. Cultivate an attitude that welcomes constructive criticism as a learning opportunity. Whether it's feedback from customers, peers, or mentors, use it to refine your approach, skillset, and strategies. **See each critique as a gift**, a free consultation on how to make your business and yourself better.

Reflect and Revise Regularly

Finally, reflection is vital for growth. Regularly pause to assess your development progress and how it's impacting your network marketing business. What's working? What isn't? Be honest with yourself and willing to make tough decisions to steer your personal advancement. **Adjust your strategies** as needed, and always keep the bigger picture in focus.

Remember, integrating personal development into your business isn't just about becoming a better entrepreneur – it's about becoming the best version of yourself. As the direct selling industry evolves, so must you. It's through this continuous cycle of learning and growth that you'll not only achieve but **sustain success**. Remain voraciously curious and relentlessly active in your development and watch as every facet of your network marketing business reaps the benefits.

Cultivating a Mindset for Network Marketing Success

As we wrap up this chapter, it's clear that **mindset is the cornerstone of success in network marketing.** By diving into the realms of positive psychology, we unearthed the power of optimism, resilience, and gratitude in propelling us towards our goals. **Developing a mindset of abundance** not only transforms how we approach challenges but also shapes our path to financial freedom.

Building Resilience for Long-Term Success

In the face of challenges, **resilience is our shield and sword**. It's the unwavering belief in our ability to bounce back stronger after setbacks.

By nurturing resilience, we can weather any storm and emerge victorious. **Resilience is not just a trait but a skill that can be honed with practice and perseverance.**

Embracing Continuous Personal Development

Our journey in is not merely about business; it's about **personal growth and evolution.** Integrating continuous personal development into our strategy is like fuel for our ambitions. It keeps us agile, adaptable, and always one step ahead. **Learning, growing, and evolving are not optional but essential for sustained success.**

In the next chapter, we delve deeper into the practical steps to harness the power of belief, resilience, and personal growth in our entrepreneurial journey. The blueprint to network marketing mastery goes beyond business - it's about nurturing a mindset that paves the way to greatness.

Chapter 5: The Blueprint for Network Marketing Achievement: Goal Setting and Execution

Erica's fingers trailed over the glossy leaves of the potted Ficus, a silent communion with life that sought sun even indoors. Rays of light stole through the blinds, painting thin lines across her desk littered with business strategies scratched into notebooks and spreadsheets awash with numbers. In the ensuite kitchen, the clink of dishes resonated as her partner, Julian, busied himself with the mundanity of cleaning up after their hastily eaten breakfast.

Her mind was a canvas on which doubts and dreams warred in vivid hues. The trill of her phone seemed to split the still morning air, calling her to the trenches of another day in the multi-level marketing world she had chosen to conquer. Sales targets danced in her head, taunting her with their mocking arithmetic, while a list of unrecruited acquaintances flickered in her peripheral vision, tangible evidence of opportunities yet untouched.

The air carried the faintest scent of lemon and detergent, a clean slate mirroring the strategy she needed to devise. Today, she vowed, would be the day she carved a path through the thicket of potential that lay unexplored at her feet. Her goal was not just to navigate this forest but to cultivate it. She mused over the pattern of past attempts, failures stitched like patchwork in her memory, each a lesson that had shaped her resolve.

Erica recalled the seminar, the one that promised to whisk away uncertainty like a magician with a flourish of his cape. Words like 'accountability' and 'tracking progress' had bounced off the walls, imbuing the room with an electric charge. They had felt then like keys to a kingdom, or perhaps more fittingly, pieces of a puzzle that could unlock the stubborn gates of success. Those mantras had since settled into the rhythm of her breath, her daily affirmations that banished whispers of defeat.

Julian appeared in the doorway, his smile a beacon. She drew on its warmth as she pondered the conversations to come, the delicate dance of persuasion that she had rehearsed in dreams and waking both. Could she weave her vision into others' aspirations, tailor motivation into a cloak they could drape around their shoulders as they marched beside her towards common goals? Her eyes locked with his, a silent plea for the courage that collective belief could kindle.

As the clock nudged her to the day's demands, Erica turned once more to her plans, the neat lines of action waiting to vibrate with the pulse of execution. What undiscovered fortitude might lie within the next phone call, the next meeting, the next shared triumph, or setback? Would today be the day she translated dreams into tangible milestones, the art of strategic planning into a symphony of orchestrated progress?

The Architect's Mindset: Crafting Your Network Marketing Empire

While financial dreams shimmer on the horizon, the routes to their realization are not laid out with glaring neon signs. They are stealth paths that must be deliberately designed, articulated with precision, and followed with unwavering commitment. MLM business owners walk the line between enthusiasm and achievement that is drawn by two unassuming, yet incredibly potent tools: **goal setting** and **strategic execution**. Navigating the competitive yet rewarding waters of network marketing requires no less than a fully equipped vessel, and with this blueprint in hand, you're about to chart a course towards undiscovered treasures of personal success and financial liberation.

Starting a network marketing business without concrete goals is akin to embarking on a voyage without a compass. Goals are the **navigational stars** guiding the entrepreneurial spirit through turbulent seas and calm waters alike. They are the benchmarks by which every decision is measured, and every action evaluated. However, merely setting goals is akin to plotting destinations without considering the currents that will carry you there. A strategic plan is the sail to your mast—it is what harnesses the winds of opportunity to propel you forward with purpose and precision.

Yet even the most detailed maps and the sturdiest vessels are meaningless without a captain who understands the art of navigation. On this entrepreneurial journey you are the captain. **Execution** is your command to the crew; it's the day-to-day steering, adjusting, and maneuvering that transform distant dots on a map into footholds of your burgeoning empire. To this end, establishing reliable systems for tracking and accountability converts the isolated process of goal pursuit into a communal voyage, reinforcing your determination and keeping the winds of diligence billowing your sails.

Embarking on this journey, you might wonder how one transitions from drafting to setting sails. The process is neither arcane nor inaccessible, but instead **a sequence of clearly defined, pragmatic steps**. These steps are the strategies you will employ, the tactics you will execute, and the milestones you will celebrate. They distill the complexity of dream realization into actionable trajectories.

Steps to Manifest Your Vision

Crafting and Conquering: A Five-Step Process for Network Marketing Triumph

At the core of this intricate dance of goal setting and accomplishment lies a rhythm that is both simple and structured - a five-step dance floor of productive endeavor.

Step 1: Set Specific Goals for Network Marketing Success

A journey of a thousand miles begins with a single, well-defined step. Your network marketing aspirations should transcend the haziness of 'success' and crystallize into figures, timelines, and tasks. It's not merely about getting more recruits; it's about **the number of lives you aim to touch** through your network month-by-month. Start by identifying where you want to be and by when, ensuring your aspirations align with the **SMART** paradigm.

Step 2: Create a Strategic Plan to Achieve Your Goals

With the stars charted, chart a course. Turn over the blueprint of your network marketing goals, and on its reverse, outline how each pinpoint will be reached. Crafts a framework that tackles the everyday: a call to be made, a presentation to be prepared, a follow-up to be completed. This finely tuned routine will be your guide, helping you keep the bigger picture in perfect focus.

Step 3: Implement Effective Execution Strategies

As the course is mapped, it's time to weigh anchor and set sail. Execution is about keeping your hands on the wheel and eyes on the horizon. Prioritize actions that amplify your efforts, cut through distractions, and capitalize on high-impact tasks. Apply tools and techniques that fine-tune your direction and pace - task management applications, time-structuring methods, and progress tracking should become your loyal deckhands.

Step 4: Track and Measure Your Results

A captain vigilant about position and progress charts a surer course. Establish metrics that serve as beacons of progress; let them reveal the journey's truth in numbers and facts. Regular analysis allows you to adjust sails and correct courses, ensuring your strategy is truly windward.

Step 5: Celebrate Your Achievements and Set New Goals

Reaching a port is not the end; it's a chance to restock, reflect, and plot the next leg of your voyage. Celebrate the milestones hard-won and let them amplify your resolve. With each achievement, the horizon expands, and so should your ambitions. Take heart in your progress and kindle the passion for the pursuits yet unborn.

The rhythm of success in network marketing abides by a cadence of precise, *implementable* actions. Walk these steps repeatedly, each cycle inching you closer to the summit of mastery. Sail on, for the wealth of worlds awaits not the timid, but the **prepared**.

Setting smart, achievable goals is the cornerstone of success in the network marketing industry. **Without a clear vision and defined objectives, it's easy to veer off course and lose sight of the ultimate goal: financial independence and prosperity.** In the realm of multi-level marketing, where the competition is fierce and the challenges are numerous, having a roadmap that outlines specific targets can make all the difference between success and stagnation.

To master the art of setting effective goals tailored to network marketing success, one must first understand the importance of specificity. Vague aspirations like "I want to be successful in network marketing" lack the clarity needed to drive purposeful action. Instead, goals should be *specific*, *measurable*, *achievable*, *relevant*, and *time-bound* - the SMART criteria.

Specificity, the 'S' in SMART, entails defining precise and unambiguous objectives. **Measurability** ensures that progress can be tracked, and achievements celebrated along the way. **Achievability** necessitates setting realistic goals that push boundaries without being unattainable. **Relevance** ensures that the goals align with your network marketing business's overall vision and mission. **Time-bound** goals have set deadlines, creating a sense of urgency and focus.

In the context of network marketing, setting SMART goals could look like establishing a target number of new recruits per month, achieving a specific sales volume within a set timeframe, or attaining a certain rank within the company by the end of the year. By breaking down these overarching objectives into smaller, actionable steps, the path to success becomes clearer and more manageable.

To further enhance goal setting in network marketing, it's crucial to tie each goal to a specific 'why'. Understanding the motivations behind the objectives can fuel determination during challenging times and serve as a constant source of inspiration on the journey towards success. Whether the goal is financial freedom, career advancement, or personal growth, having a strong 'why' can instill a sense of purpose and resilience.

Moreover, regularly reviewing and revising goals is essential in the network marketing landscape. As circumstances change, markets evolve, and new opportunities arise, being adaptable and flexible with goals allows for continuous growth and progress. **By staying agile and responsive to feedback and insights, network marketing entrepreneurs can refine their strategies and optimize their path towards success.**

[Keep reading to discover how strategic planning can turn your network marketing goals into reality.](#)

Setting clear, detailed plans and effectively executing them are crucial steps in achieving success in network marketing. Without a strategic roadmap, individuals may find themselves lost in a sea of tasks, lacking direction and purpose. By creating a roadmap tailored to their goals entrepreneurs ensure they stay on track and make steady progress towards their financial aspirations.

Strategic planning in network marketing involves breaking down overarching goals into smaller, manageable tasks. This process allows individuals to focus on specific actions that contribute to the overall success of their business. By delineating each step and assigning deadlines, network marketing professionals can ensure that they are consistently working towards their objectives.

A key aspect of effective strategic planning is adaptability. While having a detailed plan is essential, it is equally important to be flexible and able to adjust strategies as needed. The direct sales industry is constantly evolving, and being able to pivot in response to changes in the market or unforeseen obstacles is crucial for long-term success.

Successful execution of a strategic plan requires discipline and consistency. It's not enough to simply have a plan; individuals must commit to daily action every day towards their goals. By establishing daily routines and habits that align with their objectives, network marketing entrepreneurs can ensure that they are making progress, no matter how small, on a consistent basis.

**Tracking progress is essential to staying motivated and

accountable. By monitoring their performance against predefined metrics, individuals can gauge their success and identify areas for improvement. Regularly reviewing progress can also provide a sense of accomplishment and momentum, encouraging individuals to keep pushing towards their goals.

Effective execution of a strategic plan also requires prioritization. With numerous tasks vying for attention, individuals must determine what activities will have the most significant impact on their network marketing business and focus on those first. By prioritizing tasks based on their importance and relevance to their goals, entrepreneurs can optimize their productivity and efficiency.

Creating a supportive environment can also enhance the execution of a strategic plan. Surrounding oneself with like-minded individuals who share similar goals and values can provide motivation, inspiration, and accountability. By building a network of peers who can offer support and guidance, network marketing professionals can increase their chances of success and stay on track towards their objectives.

In conclusion, by developing detailed, strategic plans and executing them effectively direct sales entrepreneurs can pave the way for success in their business endeavors. Through careful planning, adaptability, consistency, and accountability, individuals can overcome obstacles and achieve their financial goals in the competitive world of network marketing.

Network Marketing Success Navigator Framework

Understanding the Foundation: Your "Why"

The Network Marketing Success Navigator Framework begins by identifying your "why" - it is the cornerstone upon which your network marketing success is constructed. Understanding the purpose behind your venture isn't just motivational; it's strategic. Recognizing your personal and professional aspirations clarifies your goals, keeping them attuned to your core values. This component acts as the compass for your network marketing journey, guiding every decision and goal you set forth. Without a firm grasp of your "why," your objectives might lack the personal significance necessary to drive you through challenging times and potentially lead you off your desired course.

SMART Goal Setting

Once your "why" is established, the framework progresses to **Setting SMART goals**. This phase is crucial; it shapes objectives that are Specific, Measurable, Achievable, Relevant, and Time-bound. Crafting such goals ensures a roadmap with clear signposts rather than a vague hope. *Specific* goals will eliminate ambiguity, *Measurable* milestones facilitate tracking progress, *Achievable* aims keep motivation alive, *Relevant* targets guarantee alignment with your larger aspirations, and *Time-bound* deadlines introduce the discipline needed to move forward with purpose.

Actionable Steps: Breaking Down the Goals

After SMART goals are set, the framework promotes breaking them down into smaller, actionable steps. This decomposition reduces the intimidation factor and creates a series of manageable tasks. It's like transforming a mountainous ascent into a series of hills, each with its own achievable peak. This modularity not only simplifies the execution but also allows for quick adaptation when circumstances change. It plays a dynamic role in moving from the planning phase to actual execution, the point where ideas begin to materialize through actions.

Crafting Your Strategic Plan

The creation of a **Strategic plan** is next, a detailed blueprint for achieving your goals. This plan is your business roadmap, indicating every turn and resource needed to reach your destination. It includes precise actions, schedules, and resource allotments. This plan not only outlines what is to be done but also provisions for the when, how, and by whom, ensuring that every aspect of your journey is thoughtfully accounted for and that the resources required are within reach.

Scheduling for Success: Prioritize and Allocate Time

An essential component is to **Prioritize and schedule** these goals within your daily life. Success in network marketing, like in any business, demands dedicated time and prioritization. This step ensures your most critical goals receive the attention they deserve and introduces a structured routine that helps in maintaining focus and consistency. Time-blocking can be a particularly effective method here, allowing you to carve out uninterrupted periods where progress can happen undisturbed.

Tracking and Accountability Systems

With your roadmap in hand, you'll move to **track and measure progress**. Establishing a robust tracking and accountability system is equivalent to placing mile markers along your route. These markers offer evidence of how far you've come and inform adjustments needed to stay on course. Regular check-ins and progress reports serve as a feedback loop, reinforcing successful behavior and highlighting areas in need of correction. This continuous monitoring is vital in maintaining the trajectory toward your goals.

Celebrate Success: Recognizing Milestones

Lastly, the framework encourages celebrating each milestone. In network marketing, the journey is as important as the destination. Recognizing your achievements with appropriate celebration reinforces your commitment and energizes you for forthcoming endeavors. Each milestone reached is a testament to your dedication and a building block in the foundation of your growing business.

In summary, the Network Marketing Success Navigator Framework offers a process model for mapping and executing your network marketing goals. It transforms the complex landscape of network marketing into an approachable progression of steps. By focusing on each part of the framework, you can navigate your network marketing business with the clarity and precision required for true success.

Through this process, tracking and accountability are not afterthoughts but integral parts of the journey, facilitating a path that is both manageable and measurable, leading you towards the realization of your entrepreneurial potential.

Now that you have delved into the core concepts of goal setting, strategic planning, and the importance of tracking progress in your business endeavors, it's time to solidify your understanding and put your newfound knowledge into action. **Remember, setting SMART goals is not just a one-time task but a continuous process that requires commitment and adaptability.**

As you craft your goals, keep them specific, measurable, achievable, relevant, and time-bound to maintain focus and ensure progress. *Strive to break down your long-term objectives into smaller, manageable tasks*, allowing you to track your advancements more effectively and stay motivated along the way.

Crafting a strategic plan is your roadmap to success in network marketing. Lean into the details, plotting out your actions step by step. **Visualize the path you need to take towards your goals**, anticipating hurdles and creating contingency plans to navigate any challenges that may arise.

Execution is the key to turning your plans into reality. Remain disciplined and consistently work towards achieving your goals. *Adapt your strategies as needed*, stay flexible, and be open to refining your approach based on results and feedback.

Accountability and tracking systems are essential for maintaining momentum. Engage with mentors, peers, or accountability partners who can keep you on track and provide valuable insights. **Regularly review your progress, celebrate achievements, and learn from setbacks**, using them as opportunities for growth.

In the ever-evolving world of direct sales, your ability to set meaningful goals, create actionable plans, execute diligently, and track progress effectively will set you apart as a leader in this thriving industry. **Embrace these principles as the foundation of your success** and watch as your network marketing journey unfolds with purpose and prosperity.

Chapter 6: Winning Customers - The Art of Product Mastery

Dawn had draped her rosy fingers over the horizon as Jonah stood on the edge of his front porch, the sky a canvas of pastel hues reflecting his mind's tumult. His heart was the battlefield of doubting whispers and staunch resolve, for today, he would dive deep into the reservoir of his knowledge to address an audience he had never faced before, armed with the conviction that his products could change lives.

The crisp morning air brushed against his skin, as if urging him toward his destiny, the same way it rustled the leaves of the old oak that stood vigil. He remembered the lessons learned under that tree, where his mentor had unfolded the secrets of storytelling, of capturing an essence so true and raw it could transform the skeptic into the believer. Those sessions, rich with anecdotes, now seemed to mingle with the morning breeze, whispering to him the power of a well-told tale.

Stepping off the porch, he felt the gravel crunch underfoot, grounding him, reminding him that each stone was like a customer—a unique entity on a path that could converge with his, if only he could map the route. This path, he mused, lay not in the grains of sand that slipped through one's fingers but in those that stayed firm within one's grip. His hands, no longer the hands of a novice but those of a sculptor, longed to shape the intangible air of influence into something as solid as the driveway beneath his feet.

As he walked through his garden, hands brushing the dew-kissed petals, his mind wandered to the crux of his speech—the point where he must unfurl the banners of his products' unique selling propositions. They were more than mere concoctions of ingredients; they were emblems of a lifestyle, a promise of transformation. Each leaf he touched seemed to stand testament to the natural wonder that he so ardently believed in. If nature could thrive with such silent eloquence, why couldn't the message of his wares burrow into hearts with equal grace?

He paused before his car, the steel beast that would accompany him to the convention center, a reluctant cocoon before the metamorphosis of his presentation. In that room awaited faces, a sea of eyes—some eager, others shut tight like clams guarding pearls of pessimism. Could he pry them open without causing harm? Could his authentic voice be the tune that resonated, turning what once was caution into curiosity?

He settled into the car seat, a temporary throne from which to ponder his next move. As the engine hummed to life, a parallel awakened in his chest - a harmony of anticipation and purpose. The streets unrolled before him; each turn an echo of the journey he navigated within. Would the path he carves today lead his listeners to see the world through his eyes, understand the need he aims to fulfill, or would they pass by it like a road not taken?

Unleash the Power of Product Mastery

Navigating the landscape of the multi-level marketing industry requires more than persistence and persuasive power; it demands a deep understanding of the products at your command. With direct sales, you're not merely selling an item; you're presenting a solution, an experience, an opportunity that can elevate the everyday for your clients. This chapter delves into the essence of product mastery, the kind of profound knowledge that instills confidence in your audience and builds the foundation of a robust customer base.

The journey to network marketing success is paved with the bricks of brand loyalty and customer satisfaction. To attain this, you must **research extensively** to not only acquaint yourself with the features and benefits of your offerings but to embody the very essence of the brand you represent.

Product knowledge is power - power to educate, to reassure, and ultimately, to persuade. Whether through personal anecdotes that breathe life into product features or crafting narratives that resonate with your target market, your aim is to forge a connection that transcends the transaction.

A network marketing strategist does not simply tout benefits but **weaves stories** that intertwine product advantages with customer needs. It's about creating a vivid picture in the minds of potential users, where they see themselves not just using a product, but benefiting from it in ways that matter to them. In this vast sea of sellers, **effective communication** stands as your lighthouse, guiding customers to the shores of your unique offering. And as you navigate these waters, it's crucial to remember that every interaction is an opportunity to reinforce your brand - your name, your integrity, your reliability.

Building a **strong personal brand** and maintaining an active online presence are no longer optional in the digital age - they are essential. As you position yourself as an authority in your field, remember that your personal brand is not just about the products you sell; it's about the values you represent and the relationships you foster. In this chapter, we explore ways to differentiate yourself in a crowded marketplace by identifying and leveraging your unique selling propositions, transforming the way potential customers see you and your business.

Comprehensive customer attraction strategies are the engines that drive business growth, yet they cannot run on enthusiasm alone. Here, you'll learn to utilize diverse marketing channels, ensuring that your message reaches the ears of those most likely to be influenced by it. From social media outreach to more intimate product demonstration events, the spectrum of engagement is broad and ripe with potential.

The Advocate's Blueprint: Enriching the Network Marketing Experience

Step 1: Research and Familiarize Yourself with Network Marketing Products

Allocate one week to immerse yourself completely in product research. Engage with your products or services, become their most knowledgeable advocate, and be prepared to share firsthand experiences. Your **authenticity** will shine through this intimate product understanding, enabling you to connect genuinely with your customers.

Step 2: Develop Effective Communication Strategies

Over the next two weeks, refine your storytelling techniques. Capture the essence of your products by creating narratives that speak to the heart of your customer's problems and aspirations. Develop **listening skills** that affirm customer concerns and testimonials that underscore product efficacy.

Step 3: Build a Strong Personal Brand and Online Presence

Dedicate a month to crafting your personal brand. Generate consistent, value-added content across selected platforms, establishing your reputation as an expert. Your USPs are your banner; display them proudly and with clarity in every piece of content you produce.

Step 4: Implement Effective Customer Attraction Strategies

Within the first quarter, actively deploy a broad spectrum of marketing tactics and observe their effectiveness. Assess engagement and optimize your strategies continually to ensure maximum visibility and attraction potential. Incentivize referrals to harness the power of word-of-mouth endorsements.

Step 5: Provide Exceptional Customer Service and Support

Commit to ongoing customer service excellence. Respond swiftly and knowledgeably to inquiries. Offer support post-purchase to demonstrate your dedication to customer success. Your aim should be a seamless service experience, infused with personal touches that turn one-time buyers into lifelong patrons.

By following these structured steps with **flexibility and dedication**, you progress towards becoming not just a salesperson, but a trusted product expert and advocate - a role indispensable in the world of network marketing. The goal is evident: to empower customers with choices that complement their lives, facilitated by your expertise and passion. Herein lies the secret to network marketing mastery: when products are understood deeply, presented passionately, and supported consistently, success is not just possible - it's inevitable.

Acquiring comprehensive product knowledge is the cornerstone of success in the competitive world of multi-level marketing (network marketing). **To become an authority in your network marketing niche, you need to immerse yourself in every aspect of the products or services offered by your company.**

Understanding the intricacies of what you are selling is crucial to effectively communicating its value to potential customers. When you possess in-depth knowledge, you exude confidence and authenticity, traits that attract customers seeking trustworthy recommendations.

By becoming a product expert, you position yourself as a reliable source of information for your customers. This expertise not only helps you sell more but also builds trust and credibility with your audience. Take the time to familiarize yourself with the ingredients, benefits, and unique selling points of the products you are promoting. Knowing how to address common questions, concerns, and objections will set you apart from those who lack this level of understanding.

Investing in your product knowledge is an investment in your success. Attend training sessions, read product guides, and engage with veteran network marketing business builders to deepen your understanding. By mastering the nuances of your products, you can tailor your pitches and recommendations to meet the specific needs of your customers. This personalized approach demonstrates care and consideration, fostering lasting relationships with your clientele.

In the dynamic world of network marketing, staying updated on product developments and industry trends is essential. Regularly seek out information, attend seminars, and participate in webinars to broaden your knowledge base. By staying ahead of the curve, you position yourself as a forward-thinker in your niche, attracting customers who value innovation and expertise. Invest in your product knowledge today to reap the rewards tomorrow.

Empower yourself with the tools and insights needed to navigate the complexities of your network marketing products with confidence. By honing your product knowledge, you not only enhance your credibility but also equip yourself with the expertise to lead thriving customer relationships. Become the go-to source for product information in your niche and watch as your customer base grows through the power of knowledge and authority.

To excel in the world of direct sales mastering the art of communication is essential. Effective storytelling and branding strategies can elevate your network marketing business by creating a strong connection with your target audience. By crafting compelling narratives around the products or services you offer, you can engage potential customers, build trust, and ultimately drive sales.

Storytelling plays a crucial role in direct sales business success. By weaving stories that resonate with your audience, you can create a powerful emotional appeal that draws them in. Share personal anecdotes about how the products have positively impacted your life or the lives of others. Highlighting real-life experiences can make the benefits of your products more tangible and relatable to your customers.

When it comes to **branding**, consistency is key. Develop a strong brand identity that reflects the values and ethos of your business. Define your unique selling proposition (USP) and communicate it consistently across all your marketing channels. Your branding should evoke a sense of trust, reliability, and quality, helping you stand out in a crowded marketplace.

Visual communication is also crucial in creating a strong brand presence. Invest in high-quality images and graphics that showcase your products in the best light. Whether it's through social media posts, website content, or marketing materials, visually appealing aesthetics can captivate your audience and leave a lasting impression.

In addition to storytelling and branding, **effective communication** involves active listening. Understand the needs and preferences of your customers by engaging in meaningful conversations. By listening attentively and addressing customer concerns, you can build stronger relationships and foster loyalty among your customer base.

To enhance your communication skills further, consider **professional development** opportunities. Attend workshops, seminars, or online courses to hone your communication techniques and stay updated on the latest marketing trends. Continuous learning and improvement are key to staying ahead in the competitive world of network marketing.

Ultimately, mastering the art of communication in network marketing involves **authenticity**. Be genuine in your interactions with customers and let your passion for your products shine through.

By building trust, engaging your audience with compelling stories, and maintaining a consistent brand identity, you can attract and retain loyal customers who believe in the value of what you offer.

The Pyramid Ascendants Framework

Acquire Product Knowledge

At the core of the Pyramid Ascendants Framework is a thorough understanding of your product. This profound knowledge base is the underpinning of your authority within the network marketing niche. It requires meticulous research into the product's features, benefits, and those compelling unique selling points that set it apart in the market. Gather information from an array of credible sources, including product manuals, user testimonials, and company resources. Knowledge is the cornerstone of credibility, and possessing it ensures you can advocate for the product with confidence and finesse. This mastery not only informs your sales approach but becomes infectious to potential customers, who are more likely to trust and buy from someone who exhibits expertise.

Develop Communication Strategies

Effective storytelling is a pivotal element in illustrating the value of network marketing products. To captivate your audience, you must weave narratives that not only connect emotionally but also posit your product as the solution to their needs. This strategy is grounded in the psychology of persuasion, harnessing the power of relatable stories that display how the product can enhance their daily lives. Articulating these messages requires authenticity and confidence, two traits that resonate with consumers seeking assurance in their purchasing decisions. Practice refining your delivery to ensure clarity and impact, always aiming to strike a chord with your prospective buyers.

Build Your Personal Brand

In the network marketing landscape, differentiation is key, and your personal brand acts as your unique signature in a crowded market. To establish this, introspectively identify your strengths, values, and the expertise that you can uniquely offer. This part of the framework is about curating an identity that resonates with your target audience and consistently reflects your association with the network marketing products. Whether you position yourself as a wellness guide, a cosmetic aficionado, or another niche expert, your personal brand should be a natural extension of who you are and what you represent.

Create a Customer Attraction Framework

A well-structured customer attraction system is essential for sustainable success in network marketing. This involves innovative tactics that may range from hosting interactive product demonstrations to utilizing social media to its fullest potential. The pivotal goal here is to design a tailored approach that resonates with your specific audience, something that grabs their attention and ignites interest. *Continuous evaluation and refinement* of your methods are necessary to adapt to changing market dynamics and consumer preferences, ensuring your strategy remains relevant and effective.

Nurture Customer Relationships

The momentum of initial attraction must transition into the cultivation of enduring relationships with customers. This aspect of the framework is about enveloping your clients in an experience that goes beyond the transactional. Providing exceptional customer service, personalized follow-ups, and ongoing education creates a nurturing environment where customers feel valued. It's here that trust is fostered, and loyalty is cemented, establishing a community around your products that thrives on genuine connections and shared values.

The Pyramid Ascendants Framework integrates these components into a cohesive strategy that evolves and adapts over time. The interplay between product knowledge, communication, personal branding, customer attraction, and relationship building is dynamic.

Every interaction feeds back into the framework, enhancing stability and resilience, and creating opportunities for ongoing development. This model not only underscores the importance of each individual element but also highlights the synergetic effect of their combined action.

By adopting this framework, you lay down a foundation equipped to keep pace with the ever-changing network marketing environment. It's a blueprint tailored for individuals who are ready to engage deeply with their products and audience, forging strong connections and crafting a distinctive path to success in the complex world of multi-level marketing.

Embrace Your Mastery in Network Marketing Products

Mastering the art of network marketing product knowledge is your gateway to success in the network marketing world. By delving deeply into the intricacies of your products or services, you position yourself as an authority in your niche, gaining the trust and respect of potential customers. **Your expertise is your greatest asset**, enabling you to communicate the value of what you offer with unwavering confidence and clarity.

Empower Your Brand through Compelling Storytelling

Effective communication lies at the heart of compelling storytelling and branding. Through the power of storytelling, you can create an emotional connection with your audience, paving the way for a lasting relationship. **Craft narratives that resonate with your customers**, highlighting not just the features of your products but also the transformational benefits they can bring into their lives.

Forge Strong Customer Connections with Unique Selling Propositions

Building a robust framework for attracting customers involves leveraging unique selling propositions. **Identify what sets your products apart** from the competition and communicate these distinct advantages in a compelling manner. By focusing on the benefits that matter most to your target audience, you can capture their attention and establish a loyal customer base.

As you continue your journey in network marketing, remember that product mastery, effective communication, and a strong customer attraction framework are the cornerstones of your success. Stay dedicated to honing your skills in these areas and watch as your business grows and flourishes.

Your commitment to excellence will set you apart as a leader in the network marketing industry, inspiring others to follow in your footsteps towards financial freedom and entrepreneurial fulfillment.

Chapter 7: Relationship Cultivation…Connect for Success

Amidst the hum of a suburban afternoon, John stood under the fledgling shade of a sycamore, his eyes flitting across the faces of potential partners and clients gathered at the neighborhood barbecue. Sunlight filtered through the leaves, casting a dappling of light and shadow across his contemplative features. In the air was the aroma of expectations, as potent as the smoky scent wafting from the grill.

He flashed a smile seasoned with the understanding that in network marketing, relationships were not just currency; they were the bedrock of a future solidified by trust and mutual benefit. The laughter of children playing tag stole through his thoughts, a gentle reminder that genuine joy could not be manufactured. He knew that his success would not be harvested from cold transactions but grown from the warmth of rapport.

The chirp of a bird drew his gaze upward momentarily; in the chatter of its song, he mirrored his own need for connection. He carried the weight of a possibility – to nurture bonds that would not only weather the challenges of business but flourish in the richness of authentic human connection. His handshake was not just a greeting; it was the seed of potential partnerships.

A whiff of freshly mown grass brought John back from the verge of abstraction, and he found himself drawn into the storytelling of a neighbor – a tale of struggle and triumph, rich with the threads of wisdom. He listened, not just to learn but to show that he was there, present in the tapestry of their experience. Amidst nods and responsive eyes, John constructed the bridge of understanding, step by step, plank by plank.

As the sun dipped lower, casting long shadows upon the gathering, John contemplated the fine art of nurturing professional relationships. The setting sun stained the sky with hues of promise, and he wondered, could the soft glow of empathy illuminate the path toward shared success as well as it lit the faces around him? Would the relationships he fostered now, under this expansive sky, be the constellation that would guide his network marketing journey?

The Key to Network Marketing Success: People Power

Success in multi-level marketing is not just about selling a product; it's deeply rooted in the relationships we cultivate along the journey. **Engaging with others** - customers, team members, and mentors - is fundamental to network marketing triumph. Person-to-person connection stands at the heart of this business model, making the ability to build trust and rapport the cornerstone for longevity and progress in the direct sales industry. **Networking is not a bonus skill**; it is an essential element that needs to be mastered and refined continuously.

Understanding the intricate dynamics of relationships, one quickly realizes the immense potential lying within every conversation, meeting, and social connection. **Trust and rapport** are not just nice-to-haves; they are the fuel that powers the engine of network marketing businesses. This chapter is dedicated to teaching you how to solidify these aspects, showing that when trust and rapport are in place, sales and growth often follow naturally.

The focus here is not merely on building a network but on nurturing a web of professional relationships, each filled with mutual respect and potential for growth.

The Art of Network Building

To excel in network marketing, it's essential to **develop top-tier networking skills** - skills that go beyond the basics of adding contacts on social media or exchanging business cards. It is about fostering meaningful conversations, actively listening to your peers, and providing value in every interaction. This section aims to empower readers with tactics and strategies to become networking maestros, adept at finding and creating opportunities in every handshake.

In the world of network marketing, the standard pitch is an outdated tool; here, engaged dialogue reigns supreme. As such, understanding the significance of interpersonal connections becomes paramount. This chapter will guide you in transforming every encounter into a lasting partnership, showing how trust is the very foundation on which successful network marketing careers are built.

Nurturing Professional Relationships

The journey toward network marketing mastery is not one of solitary triumphs but of collective victory. **Cultivating techniques** to enrich and maintain professional relationships is a vital strategy for anyone looking to sustain a flourishing network marketing business. This section delves into the methodologies behind strong relationship maintenance, ensuring that your team is not just vast but also robust.

Here, actionable insights revolve around communication excellence, conflict resolution, and consistent follow-ups, all geared to help readers forge alliances that withstand the test of time. Learning to navigate the network marketing relationship web is not just about expanding one's business but also about *enriching the professional environment for all involved*.

In synthesizing these key principles, this chapter provides a clear pathway for network marketing enthusiasts to harness the power of relationships effectively. It offers a comprehensive approach to network marketing success that reaches beyond individual accomplishment and into the realm of collaborative prosperity. Through these lessons, one can become not just a participant in the industry but a respected leader, valued for the depth and quality of their connections.

Whether you're a seasoned network marketing professional or a newcomer eager to make your mark, the insights within these pages are designed to equip you with the relationship-building prowess required for lasting success. The wisdom gleaned from here is poised to become an indispensable part of your toolkit, positioning you to not only navigate the complexities of this dynamic field but to excel within it.

As we venture through the layers of interaction that form the fabric of network marketing success, remember that it is in the genuine moments of connection where true growth and achievement are found. When you strengthen the relationships within your network, you elevate not just your business, but the entire community.

Building and maintaining relationships is the cornerstone of success in the multifaceted world of direct sales. **Developing top-tier networking skills is pivotal for your success** in this industry. Networking goes beyond merely exchanging business cards at events; it involves creating genuine connections based on trust and mutual benefit. In multi-level marketing, your network is your net worth, and the quality of your relationships directly influences your business growth and sustainability.

To excel in this industry, you must cultivate a diverse network that includes potential customers, team members, mentors, and industry peers. **Effective networking requires active listening, clear communication, and a genuine interest in others**. Engage in meaningful conversations to understand the needs and goals of those you interact with. In network marketing, success is not solely about selling products but about building relationships that lead to long-term success and loyalty.

Participating in industry events, networking groups, and online communities can help expand your network and create valuable connections. **Being consistent in your interactions and nurturing relationships over time is key**.

Networking is not a one-time effort but an ongoing process that requires dedication and authenticity. Remember, in network marketing, the connections you make today could lead to opportunities tomorrow.

Seek out mentors and influencers within the network marketing industry who can provide guidance and support. Learning from those who have achieved success in network marketing can offer valuable insights and help you avoid common pitfalls. Building relationships with experienced individuals in the field can accelerate your growth and provide a roadmap to navigate the complexities of network marketing.

In direct sales, networking is not about transactional exchanges but about **building genuine connections based on trust and shared values**. Authenticity is crucial in network marketing, as people are more likely to do business with those they trust and relate to on a personal level. Invest time in getting to know your network on a deeper level, understanding their needs, preferences, and aspirations to tailor your approach and build lasting relationships.

As you embark on your journey in network marketing, remember that **developing top-tier networking skills is essential** for your success. Take the time to build meaningful relationships, listen attentively, and offer value to others in your network. By cultivating a strong and diverse network, you pave the way for long-term success and growth in the dynamic world of network marketing.

Elevate your networking skills to new heights and uncover the secrets to thriving in the Network Marketing industry.

Building trust and rapport in network marketing is not just a beneficial strategy; it's an essential cornerstone of success in the industry. **Long-standing customer relationships** are the lifeblood of any network marketing business, providing a solid foundation for growth and sustainability.

Trust is the currency of these relationships, earned through honesty, consistency, and integrity in all interactions. When customers trust you, they are more likely to become repeat buyers, refer others to your business, and even join your team as distributors.

Establishing and maintaining trust with your customers requires a **focus on authenticity** and genuine connection. Showcasing your passion for the products or services you offer, being transparent in your business practices, and always putting the customer's needs first are key components of building trust.

Consistent communication that is personalized and attentive further solidifies this trust, showing customers that you value their support and are committed to their satisfaction.

Rapport, on the other hand, goes beyond trust and enters the realm of genuine connection. **Building rapport** with customers involves creating a sense of familiarity, understanding, and mutual respect. This can be achieved through active listening, empathetic communication, and a genuine interest in the well-being of your customers. By fostering a positive and friendly relationship with your customer base, you not only increase loyalty but also pave the way for deeper engagement and collaboration.

In the direct sales industry, where relationships drive success, **nurturing long-standing customer connections** is a top priority. Beyond the initial sale, it's crucial to continue investing in these relationships through follow-ups, personalized recommendations, and ongoing support. By demonstrating your commitment to their satisfaction and success, you not only retain existing customers but also create advocates who will champion your business to others.

Remember, in the world of network marketing, success is not just about making a sale; it's about **building a community** of loyal customers and team members who believe in your vision and trust in your expertise. By prioritizing trust and rapport in your customer relationships, you lay a solid foundation for long-term success in the network marketing industry. Each interaction is an opportunity to strengthen these connections and foster a network of supporters who are not just customers but partners in your journey towards financial freedom and entrepreneurial success.

Building Effective Communication Skills

Effective communication serves as the foundation for nurturing professional relationships within the network marketing industry. Equipping oneself with the ability to clearly express ideas, listen actively, and respond appropriately is essential. To hone these skills, focus on developing an empathetic listening approach, where understanding the perspective of others becomes a priority.

Additionally, strive to be articulate when conveying your own messages, ensuring that your points are succinct, and your intentions are transparent. Engaging in regular communication training, such as attending workshops or practicing with a mentor, can strengthen these abilities and position you as a leader who values and fosters open dialogue.

Foster Emotional Intelligence

Emotional intelligence (EI) is critical in managing personal emotions and understanding those of others, especially in an environment as dynamic as network marketing. Cultivate your EI by practicing self-awareness, self-regulation, motivation, empathy, and social skills. This not only aids in building rapport but also in conflict resolution and team motivation. By showing genuine concern for the well-being and success of your team members and clients, you deepen the trust and reinforce the relational bonds that are vital for long-term success in the network marketing industry.

Encourage Peer-to-Peer Mentoring

Peer-to-peer mentoring can significantly enhance the relational fabric of your network marketing network. Encourage seasoned members to share insights and experiences with newer ones. Establishing a culture of mentorship within your team promotes a sense of community, fosters collective learning, and accelerates the professional growth of all members. Through this reciprocal exchange of knowledge, team members gain not only skills but also confidence, which is instrumental in cultivating a robust professional network.

Provide Value Beyond Products

In network marketing, relationships should not be transactional. Aim to provide value to your customers and team members beyond just the products or business opportunity at hand. Offer educational content, training, and personal development resources that empower individuals to grow their skill sets. Facilitating access to these resources demonstrates that you have a genuine interest in their holistic success and are invested in more than mere financial gain, which can strengthen loyalty and engagement.

Celebrate Success and Recognize Efforts

Recognition plays a powerful role in fostering a positive network marketing community. Celebrate the milestones and successes of your team members publicly, whether it be through social media shoutouts, awards, or acknowledgment during group meetings. Additionally, recognize their efforts, not just outcomes. This encourages continued participation and effort, and it lets your team know that their contributions are valued, regardless of scale.

Create Opportunities for Social Interaction

Networking events and social gatherings are instrumental in deepening bonds within your network marketing circle. Create opportunities for your team to interact in informal settings, where they can build relationships without the pressure of sales or recruitment. Team retreats, social media groups, and local meetups can provide relaxed environments that foster camaraderie and allow members to connect on a more personal level.

Embrace Technological Tools for Relationship Management

In today's digital age, leveraging technology to manage and strengthen relationships is indispensable. Utilize CRM (Customer Relationship Management) systems to keep track of interactions, preferences, and progress of your customers and team members.

Social media platforms can also be powerful tools for maintaining connection and engagement. Regular, personalized communication through these channels can make your professional network feel valued and informed.

Continuously Learn and Adapt

The direct sales industry is ever evolving, and so are the techniques for relationship management within it. Stay informed about the latest trends in communication, networking, and personal development. Attend industry conferences, participate in webinars, and read relevant literature to continually refine your approach. As you adapt and integrate new strategies, you not only set yourself up for success but also inspire your network to follow suit, reinforcing a culture of continuous learning and improvement.

Remember, the strongest professional relationships in direct sales are those that are mutually enriching and are sustained through dedicated effort. Implement these techniques with consistency and watch as your network transforms into a thriving community anchored by trust, camaraderie, and shared success.

Building strong relationships and networking effectively are the cornerstones of success in the network marketing industry. **Mastering top-tier networking skills** is not an option but a necessity for thriving in this competitive field. The ability to connect with diverse individuals, from customers to mentors, is a skill that can be honed through practice and dedication. By understanding the significance of **trust** and **rapport** in every interaction, network marketing entrepreneurs can lay the foundation for long-lasting and fruitful relationships. Trust is the currency of the network marketing world, and without it, success becomes elusive.

In the realm of network marketing, the power of **professional relationships** cannot be underestimated. Every connection made has the potential to catalyze growth and drive business success. It is essential to cultivate techniques for **nurturing and enriching** these relationships continually. From engaging in active listening to showing genuine interest in others' success, every interaction is an opportunity to strengthen the web of connections that support your network marketing journey. Remember, in this business, your network is your net worth.

As you navigate the network marketing landscape, keep in mind that every relationship you build contributes to the fabric of your success.

Invest time in understanding your customers and team members on a personal level. Show empathy, provide value, and always deliver on your promises. Consistency is key in maintaining trust and loyalty. By being authentic and transparent in your dealings, you not only foster strong connections but also set the stage for sustainable growth in your network marketing business.

In the multifaceted world of network marketing, building relationships is not just a strategy but a way of life. It is through genuine connections, built on trust and mutual respect, that the true essence of network marketing shines. Embrace the power of networking, prioritize trust and rapport in all interactions, and commit to nurturing your professional relationships with care and dedication. As you continue your network marketing journey, remember that success is not just about sales numbers but about the meaningful connections you forge along the way.

Chapter 8: Leading the Vanguard...Inspiring the Masses

Beneath the simmering skyline of a bustling metropolis, Mark navigated through the throng of city dwellers, a solitary captain sailing through a sea of anonymity. His mind churned with the same restlessness that animated the streets; there lay before him a sprawling network of individuals each chasing their own version of success.

He belonged to a world whispered about in skeptical tones - a multi-level marketing empire built upon the promise of prosperity and the lure of leadership. Yet, as he brushed past the shoulders of strangers, an unsettling truth gnawed at him – to guide and grow his team required more than the charisma that had rocketed him to the upper echelons, it required a genuine transformation.

Around him, the city hummed, and he could almost hear the heartbeats of the multitude, a cacophony of aspirations that mirrored his own inner tumult. Mark once believed that fervor and a well-spun narrative could marshal an army of sellers beneath him, but the fallout of turnover and lost trust had begun to erode his confidence. Where had he faltered? And how could he forge a path of mutual success in an environment that seemed so intrinsically competitive?

The quick click of heels on pavement, the subtle dance of light and shadow on the high-rises, all served to remind him that leadership was an art juxtaposed upon the canvas of reality. It dawned on him that his team was not a mere extension of his ambition but a collective of individual dreams, each requiring nourishment and direction. It was in the art of connection and the sharing of vulnerabilities that the seeds of empowerment would sprout. Could he learn the language of mentorship that spoke not only to goals but also to the spirit?

With every stride, Mark let the ambient cityscape wash over him, the breeze whispering like a cohort of voices from those in his charge, urging him towards a deeper introspection. He had sought to transform his team from the outside, yet it was his own transformation that beckoned - a metamorphosis into a leader not just dressed in success, but also robed in empathy and strength.

As dusk approached, and the sky painted itself in hues of resignation, Mark stood at a crossroads lit by the fading glow of the day and the nascent twinkle of streetlamps. There, surrounded by lives in motion, he felt the embryonic stirrings of a communal triumph, a path paved by collective tenacity. A leader not as a towering figure but as a guiding star.

Would Mark's newfound resolve sculpt an edifice of shared victories, or would the temptations of his past ways cast long shadows over the future he aimed to build?

Unleashing the Leader Within: Charting the Path to Inspiring Success

The journey to the apex of the multi-level marketing hierarchy is fraught with challenges that demand more than just individual finesse; they require **inspiring leadership and a cohesive team**. At the core of every successful network marketing enterprise lies a leader who is not just a savvy entrepreneur but a catalyst for collective achievement.

This adept navigator doesn't simply sail their own ship but teaches others to harness the winds of commerce and navigate the waters of market opportunity. As you delve into the intricacies of leading the network marketing vanguard, one principle rings true: the power to inspire and mobilize a team is the greatest asset in your entrepreneurial arsenal.

Leadership in network marketing is an art that blends **vision, motivation, and strategic action**. It's about uncovering the intrinsic qualities that make a leader magnetic, attracting and retaining a committed team. The mission is clear: to cultivate a legion of individuals who are as invested in the ascent to network marketing mastery as you are. Each leader stands at the helm, the quintessential embodiment of the values and work ethic that define their group's identity. As you strive to develop these aspects in yourself, the transformation from a solitary player to a revered leader unfolds, offering a blueprint to the empowerment of every member in your cohort.

Taking the reins involves more than just the knowledge of your product or service; it is about fostering an **environment of mutual success**. Implementing team-building strategies isn't just about growth numbers - it's a careful choreography of instilling confidence, nurturing skills, and expanding the collective horizons of your team. This chapter peels back the layers to reveal the mechanics of constructing a network marketing ecosystem where every individual thrives spurred by collective ambition and individual empowerment.

Turning toward motivational currents, this discourse **empowers you to be the mentor** your team needs. Through potent mentorship and unwavering support, you will not only guide your team but also instigate a ripple effect of leadership.

Your charges will learn not just to operate within your framework, but to innovate and mentor those in their wake. The transformation from followers to autonomous leaders writes the real success story of any network marketing endeavor and sets the stage for a culture of self-propagating growth and education.

The Vanguard Formula: Igniting Leadership Potential

Step 1: Develop Leadership Qualities

Launching this transformative journey begins with a mirror—one that reflects the leader you aspire to be. Cultivating self-awareness and emotional intelligence is the stone upon which leadership is sharpened. By understanding and managing both your emotions and those of others, you set a precedent of leading with empathy, the glue that bonds you to your team. Commit to **lifelong learning**, adopt leadership principles from the pantheon of network marketing greats, and above all you must lead by example, exhibiting the **integrity, accountability, and work ethic** you envision for your team.

Step 2: Implement Effective Team-Building Strategies

Protect this ethos by instilling a clear vision and mission within your team - a vision that aligns with overall aspirations yet resonates personally with every member. The onus is on you to **foster a culture of inclusion and collaboration**, where ideas fuse and strategies emerge from the collective intelligence. Recognition plays a pivotal role in this milieu, as a team celebrated is a team motivated.

Step 3: Provide Mentorship and Support

The fabric of your network marketing dynasty will be woven with the threads of individual growth and development. As a mentor, your role transcends simple oversight; take it upon yourself to equip your disciples with the tools to expand their skills and finesse their strategies. Offering **one-on-one coaching and skill-building workshops**, while encouraging autonomy, will sculpt not merely followers but future leaders in their own rite.

Step 4: Communicate Effectively

The bedrock of effective leadership is communication—open, empathetic, and tailored to individual needs. Give rise to a culture where your team feels seen and heard, where their contributions are not just acknowledged but **actively integrated**. Adapt your communication, be it through face-to-face interactions or digital correspondence, to align with the nuances of each team member's style and preference.

Step 5: Motivate and Inspire Your Team

Unearth the unique motivations that drive each team member. Individuals respond to distinct cues; recognizing this can turn a generic incentive into a **personal catalyst for growth and achievement**.

By embodying the success you advocate, you become the standard-bearer of success, inspiring your team not with words alone, but with tangible achievements and opportunities for advancement within the network marketing pantheon.

This formula, while sequential, is not rigid - it thrives on reflexivity, adapting to the changing dynamics of teams and the market. It's an iterative process, always active, always striving for better. The end goal is clear: a team of empowered individuals, each a leader in their domain, collectively pushing the boundaries toward unprecedented network marketing success.

Your charge is clear: establish these principles as the fundamental truth of your leadership doctrine. As you step forward, remember that mentorship isn't simply a role - it's the legacy you leave within your network and the **footprints that lead the way to multi-level marketing mastery**.

In multi-level marketing leadership qualities play a pivotal role in guiding and growing a successful team. To excel in network marketing requires more than just individual effort; it demands the ability to inspire, motivate, and empower others towards collective success. As you progress in your network marketing journey, honing your leadership skills becomes indispensable for fostering a culture of collaboration and achievement within your organization.

One of the key leadership qualities necessary for guiding and growing your network marketing team is **empathy**. Understanding the motivations, challenges, and aspirations of your team members allows you to connect with them on a deeper level. By demonstrating empathy, you create a supportive environment where individuals feel valued and understood, paving the way for enhanced teamwork and productivity.

Alongside empathy, effective communication is another vital leadership quality. Clear, timely, and open communication fosters trust among team members and facilitates the smooth flow of information and ideas. By articulating your vision, expectations, and feedback concisely, you set a foundation for transparent dialogue and collaboration within your network marketing team.

Leadership in network marketing also requires resilience. Challenges, setbacks, and obstacles are inevitable on the path to success. A resilient leader remains steadfast in the face of adversity, showing unwavering determination and perseverance. By embodying resilience, you inspire your team to overcome obstacles, stay focused on goals, and navigate through turbulent times with confidence.

Furthermore, a great network marketing leader exhibits **adaptability**. The business landscape is dynamic, requiring leaders to adjust strategies, embrace change, and seize opportunities swiftly. Being adaptable enables you to pivot, when necessary, capitalize on emerging trends, and lead your team towards continuous growth and innovation.

Effective decision-making is a hallmark of strong leadership in network marketing. Decisive leaders assess situations, gather relevant information, weigh choices, and make informed decisions promptly. By exercising good judgment and taking calculated risks, you instill confidence in your team and guide them towards decisive actions that drive success.

Building leadership qualities to guide and grow your network marketing team is a continuous process of learning, reflection, and improvement. By fostering empathy, honing communication skills, embodying resilience, embracing adaptability, and making effective decisions, you set the stage for inspiring, motivating, and empowering your team towards collective achievement.

Implement team-building strategies that create an environment of mutual success so that your business success doesn't just hinge on your individual efforts but also on the collaborative strength of a well-built team.

Implementing team-building strategies that foster a culture of mutual success is paramount for sustainable growth and achievement within the network marketing landscape. Building a cohesive and motivated team is not just about recruiting members but also about nurturing and empowering them to reach their full potential.

Effective team building starts with clear communication and shared goals. **Establishing a platform for open communication** where team members feel heard and valued is crucial. Regular meetings, both in person and virtually, can provide a space for team members to voice their ideas, concerns, and achievements.

Creating a sense of community within the team fosters trust and camaraderie, essential elements for a thriving network marketing organization.

Setting clear objectives and roles within the team is also fundamental. Each team member should understand their responsibilities and how they contribute to the overarching goals of the group. By delineating roles and expectations, individuals can work together cohesively towards a shared vision of success.

Encouraging a sense of accountability within the team ensures that everyone is committed to their tasks and supports one another in meeting objectives.

Promoting a culture of continuous learning is another key aspect of team building. Providing opportunities for training, skill development, and personal growth cultivates a dynamic and motivated team. As a leader in network marketing, it's essential to **offer mentorship and guidance** to team members, helping them navigate challenges and capitalize on opportunities for advancement. **Encouraging a growth mindset** within the team fosters innovation and adaptation, vital qualities in a rapidly evolving market.

Recognizing and celebrating achievements within the team is essential for morale and motivation. Acknowledging individual and collective successes reinforces a culture of appreciation and inspires continued effort towards shared goals. By **building a supportive and uplifting environment**, team members feel motivated to excel and contribute to the overall success of the network marketing organization.

In conclusion, **implementing team-building strategies** that prioritize communication, shared goals, clear roles, continuous learning, mentorship, recognition, and support are foundational for creating a prosperous and harmonious network marketing team. By fostering a culture of collaboration, mutual respect, and shared success, network marketing leaders can inspire their team members to reach new heights and achieve collective prosperity.

The Framework of Network Marketing Leadership

Identify Your Leadership Qualities

The cornerstone of any robust network marketing leadership framework begins with a thorough self-assessment to understand the strengths and weaknesses in your leadership qualities. Critical attributes such as proficient communication skills, high-level empathy, adaptability, adept problem-solving, and a resilient growth mindset form the foundation of effective network marketing guidance.

Assess your existing skill set and commit to a targeted plan for development and enhancement. *Recognizing your leadership posture* not only positions you to leverage your innate strengths but also illuminates the path to bolstering areas requiring growth. This self-awareness allows for a nuanced approach to leadership within the industry and sets the stage for the cultivation of an empowered team.

Implement Team-Building Strategies

Creating an environment conducive to mutual success necessitates the implementation of deliberate team-building strategies. Environments that thrive are marked by open communication channels, clearly defined expectations, a spirit of collaboration, and recognition of team successes. Consider developing systems that **encourage team interaction** and foster a culture where support and empowerment are the norms. As a lynchpin of the network marketing leadership structure, these strategies are not static but require continuous refinement to adapt to the team's ever-evolving dynamics. Establishing these supportive systems positions team members to work cohesively towards common goals, maximizing the potential for collective achievement.

Mentorship and Empowerment

Effective mentorship circles back to the core of inspiring network marketing teams - guidance, support, and access to critical resources. Actively engaging in active listening, offering constructive feedback, and crafting opportunities for personal and professional development can significantly uplift team members.

Empowerment arises when individuals feel equipped and energized to take charge of their success, supported by the mentorship tools you provide. This element of the framework is about translating potential into action, enabling team members to progress independently with confidence, backed by the knowledge that mentorship is a call away.

Lead by Example

The adage "actions speak louder than words" resonates profoundly within this framework. By actively embodying the leadership qualities you value, you transmit a powerful message to your team. Transparency, ethics, a commendable work ethic, alongside vulnerability and openness to feedback are aspects that underline credible leadership. Ripples of influence from **leading by example** resonate through your team, inspiring members to mirror these commendable traits. In essence, your conduct paves the path for establishing behavioral benchmarks within your team.

Continuous Development

In an ever-changing industry like network marketing, stagnation is the antithesis of leadership. Prioritizing continuous personal and professional growth is what distinguishes good leaders from great ones. Investing in learning opportunities, staying abreast of industry trends, and engaging in professional development initiatives ensures that your leadership toolkit is always expanding.

This proactive approach not only fortifies your leadership capacity but also signals to your team the importance of **lifelong learning** as a value within the organization. By modeling this commitment, leaders instill in their teams the same thirst for knowledge and improvement, cultivating a culture that values progression.

In synthesizing the components of the Keystone Framework, each aspect interlocks to support the structural integrity of your network marketing leadership. This conceptual model is not merely a collection of abstract ideas but presents symbiotic elements that function cooperatively.

As you embed the identified qualities into your leadership practice, they naturally segue into the application of team-building strategies that not only construct but sustain a thriving team environment.

As the framework is applied, mentorship becomes the operative tool to amplify team capabilities, empowering members to aspire to their entrepreneurial zeniths. Leadership by example operates as a centrifugal force, exerting a steady influence that shapes team culture. All this, while a dedication to continuous development, ensures that your leadership approach remains dynamic, adaptive, and resilient in the face of network marketing's shifting marketplace.

Applying the Keystone Framework is an ongoing journey of refinement and adaptation. There are always new heights to scale, additional wisdom to absorb, and fresh challenges to conquer. As you integrate these principles and strategies into your leadership, you not only elevate your abilities but also fortify the foundation upon which your network marketing success is built.

Summary: Leading the Network Marketing Vanguard

Throughout this chapter, we have explored the critical importance of **leadership qualities** in network marketing. A successful direct sales business is not just about individual effort but also about guiding and nurturing a team towards collective success. By understanding the core tenets of effective leadership, **implementing team-building strategies**, and **empowering team members through mentorship**, you can pave the way for a thriving network marketing organization.

Looking Ahead: A Culture of Collaboration

As you progress in your network marketing journey, remember that your success is intricately linked to the success of your team. Cultivating a culture of collaboration is not just about boosting your own sales but about lifting the entire team towards greater heights. By honing your leadership skills, creating a supportive team environment, and offering mentorship to those under your wing, you can foster a sense of unity and drive that propels everyone towards success.

Take Action: Steps for Immediate Application

1. **Lead by example**: Show your team the dedication and hard work required to succeed in network marketing.
2. **Communicate effectively**: Keep an open line of communication to ensure everyone is on the same page.
3. **Provide guidance and support**: Be a mentor figure for your team members, offering advice and encouragement when

needed.
4. **Celebrate wins together**: Acknowledge and celebrate the achievements of individuals within your team to boost morale and motivation.
5. **Continuously improve**: Never stop learning and growing as a leader, as your development directly impacts the success of your team.

In the next chapter, we will delve into the importance of **effective communication** in network marketing and how mastering this skill can elevate your business to new heights. Stay tuned as we unravel the intricacies of connecting with your audience and team members in meaningful ways.

Chapter 9: Cultivate Your Inner Strengths

Even at the zenith of prosperity, the weight of the world can press cold and heavy. So found Stella, knee-deep in her ascent up the network marketing ranks, her desk awash in streams of daylight that painted her success in a glaring, unrelenting hue. Her fingers danced across the keyboard; an orchestrated chaos of ambition interwoven with hesitance. Each click whispered promises of a future as bright as the noonday sun that filtered through her home office window. Yet behind her eyes, a cavalcade of doubts played their somber melody.

A sigh slipped from Stella's lips, dissipating into the fragrance of freshly ground coffee that lingered from the morning's first, and only, comforting cup. "Resilience," she murmured to herself, rolling the word in her mouth like a morsel of sustenance to feed her wavering spirit. The highs and lows of her industry were notoriously capricious, yet her mind sought the steady rhythm of resilience, a drumbeat to march to through the labyrinth of uncertainty.

She recalled the stern face of her mentor, whose words were graven on her memory: "Your character, Stella, is forged at the anvil of adversity. Master your mind, and the forge's fire will not consume you but rather illuminate your path." How often had she clung to that wisdom, the thought a fulcrum upon which she balanced her aspirations and anxieties with equal care?

Lunchtime traffic hummed softly beyond the confines of her sanctuary. A knock at her door jolted her from introspection, and she welcomed the interjection, if only to stifle the arduous dialogue within. In the corner of her eye, she spied the novel she'd been reading - its protagonist's journey through trials of the heart not unlike her trials of the spirit. It lay open, a silent testament to the solace found in parallel struggles.

How often had she neglected her own well-being on this odyssey, she wondered? The reflection sparked a minuscule rebellion, a desire to step beyond the charts and figures, the network strategies, and sales pitches, into a world where she remembered the essence of her humanity. Just as a heartbeat stronger after rest, might her entrepreneurial fervor not surge anew upon the pillars of self-care?

The day waned, her office awash in shadows that crept beneath the door, unnoticed by Stella as she pondered the possibility of a tomorrow unburdened by today's doubts. For if resilience and mindset mastery were her crafts, was she not the artisan of her own fate, capable of sculpting a reality both prosperous and peaceful?

What will she decide to shape next, and how will the tools of resilience and self-care redefine her journey?

Turn Setbacks into Comebacks

The true mettle of a network marketing entrepreneur is not determined by how they revel in success, but by how they navigate the troughs of trials and tribulations. Resilience is not a luxury in this line of work; it's a non-negotiable skill for those determined to ascend the pyramid of success. **Building a resilient mindset** is akin to constructing an unshakeable foundation for your network marketing enterprise. This foundation endures the relentless waves of challenge and change inherent in the landscape.

Within these paragraphs lays a blueprint for resilience that transcends basic motivation, veering into the realm of psychological endurance and emotional intelligence. Aspiring network marketing leaders must learn to **foster a resilient mindset** to weather the industry's volatility—an industry peppered with both dazzling triumphs and daunting setbacks. It's about molding a mindset receptive to learning, adaptable to change, and unwavering in the face of adversity.

Mindset mastery techniques are your arsenal for maintaining laser-focus and drive. These techniques are not mere platitudes but are battle-tested strategies drawn from the experiences of top industry performers. They offer a clear path to amplify your concentration and bolster your entrepreneurial spirit. By **implementing these techniques**, entrepreneurs can create a mental sanctum that fends off distractions and maintains progress towards their business goals, even when headwinds are strong.

Prioritizing self-care and mental well-being is often glossed over in the entrepreneurial narrative, dismissed as ancillary in the face of 'more important' business activities. However, neglecting this critical backbone of entrepreneurial resilience is tantamount to undermining the very structure on which your network marketing success is built. Self-care is the silent guardian of your mental fortitude, refreshing your mind, recharging your spirit, and preparing you for the ongoing journey.

Forge the Unyielding Entrepreneurial Spirit

The network marketing industry's oscillating nature demands not just psychological resilience but the cultivation of an *entrepreneurial spirit* that is at once flexible and steadfast. This spirit is the lifeblood of network marketing success, encapsulating the drive and passion necessary to innovate, inspire, and influence - a trifecta of abilities essential for creating a prosperous network marketing business. To nurture this spirit, one must consistently engage in practices that sharpen the mind, inspire creativity, and maintain health.

Resilient entrepreneurs understand that setbacks are simply *setups for a comeback*. Every moment of failure is ripe with insights, each struggle is fraught with valuable lessons, and every rejection has the potential to fuel your climb to the top. Accepting and learning from these experiences build both your acumen and your arsenal, making you a force to be reckoned with in the competitive world of network marketing.

Sustaining the Entrepreneurial Journey

In the thick of challenges, the importance of community becomes undeniably clear. network marketing thrives on the strength of its networks, and by **engaging in community enhancement**, entrepreneurs not only contribute to the well-being of others but also fortify their own support systems. This reciprocal reinforcement creates a tightly knit fabric of resilience that supports each individual, even as they strive for personal success.

Moreover, **taking the initiative in self-improvement** is a hallmark of the zealous entrepreneur. Active growth and development are not passive pursuits; they are deliberate, strategic actions taken daily. Whether through professional training, educating oneself about the latest market trends, or adopting new business practices, the process of continuous improvement solidifies one's position in the network marketing hierarchy and guards against the ever-looming threat of stagnation.

In sum, this chapter is a clarion call to network marketing entrepreneurs to *empower themselves* beyond the mundane pursuit of profits. It vibrates with the message that true mastery over the network marketing domain emerges when one's inner fortitude aligns with professional prowess. Engage with this journey of resilience-building, mindset mastery, and self-nurturing to unlock levels of sustained network marketing success that are not merely aspirational but wholly attainable.

Building a resilient mindset is a crucial component of navigating the unpredictable landscape of the network marketing industry. The highs and lows that come with entrepreneurial ventures can test one's mental strength and resolve. To thrive in the face of challenges, it is essential to cultivate a mindset that can weather setbacks and adapt to changing circumstances. **Resilience is not just about bouncing back; it's about bouncing forward, using adversity as a steppingstone to growth and success.**

In network marketing, rejection and criticism are common experiences that can wear down even the most determined individuals. **It is crucial to develop a mindset that can withstand the sting of rejection and learn from setbacks rather than letting them define your journey.** Resilience in direct sales involves maintaining a positive attitude in the face of adversity, believing in your abilities, and staying committed to your goals despite obstacles along the way.

One key aspect of fostering resilience is maintaining a growth mindset. This mindset acknowledges that failures and challenges are opportunities for learning and growth rather than signs of incompetence. By embracing a growth mindset, network marketing entrepreneurs can approach setbacks with a sense of curiosity and a willingness to adapt and improve.

Self-awareness is another essential element of building resilience in network marketing. Understanding your strengths, weaknesses, and triggers allows you to navigate challenges more effectively and seek support when needed. By cultivating self-awareness, you can better manage stress, regulate your emotions, and make decisions that align with your values and goals.

Embracing resilience is not about avoiding difficulties, but about facing them head-on with grace and determination.

By fostering a resilient mindset, network marketing entrepreneurs can navigate the highs and lows of the industry with confidence and poise. Through self-awareness, growth mindset, and a positive attitude, individuals can build the mental and emotional strength needed to overcome obstacles and achieve long-term success in their entrepreneurial endeavors.

In the fast-paced world of multi-level marketing (network marketing), maintaining focus and drive is essential for long-term success. Implementing mindset mastery techniques can help you stay on track and navigate the challenges that come with running your own business. One key strategy for maintaining focus is to set clear goals and create a roadmap to achieve them. **By clearly defining your objectives and outlining the steps needed to reach them**, you can stay motivated and on course even when faced with obstacles.

Another crucial aspect of mindset mastery is the practice of positive visualization. Visualizing your success, imagining achieving your goals, and picturing the life you desire can help boost your motivation and drive. **Take time each day to visualize your success**, focusing on the emotions and rewards that come with achieving your goals. This practice can help reinforce your belief in your abilities and keep you motivated during challenging times.

Mindset mastery also involves cultivating a growth mindset. Instead of viewing challenges as obstacles, **see them as opportunities for growth**. Embrace a mindset of continuous learning and improvement, and approach setbacks as valuable learning experiences rather than insurmountable roadblocks. **By adopting a growth mindset**, you can stay resilient and adaptable in the face of adversity, allowing you to bounce back stronger than ever.

In addition to setting goals, visualizing success, and cultivating a growth mindset, it's important to establish a routine that supports your mental and emotional well-being. **Incorporate daily practices such as meditation, exercise, journaling, and self-reflection** to help you stay centered and focused. **Taking care of your mental health is crucial for long-term success in network marketing**, as it allows you to approach challenges with a clear and positive mindset.

Surround yourself with a supportive community of like-minded individuals who can provide encouragement, advice, and motivation. **Engaging with a network of peers in the network marketing industry can help you stay inspired and connected**, providing a sense of camaraderie and shared purpose. **Regularly engaging with your community can boost your morale and keep you motivated**, even during tough times.

Remember that mindset mastery is an ongoing process. It requires dedication, perseverance, and a commitment to personal growth. **Stay open to new ideas, techniques, and strategies** that can help you enhance your mindset and drive towards success in network marketing. By consistently working on your mindset and staying focused on your goals, you can navigate the highs and lows of the network marketing industry with resilience and determination.

The Pillar of Entrepreneurial Success: Self-Care and Mental Well-being

Entrepreneurial resilience is not merely about enduring the inevitable struggles that come with the network marketing industry - it's about maintaining your mental and emotional health to thrive amidst those challenges. Prioritizing self-care is an essential strategy for any entrepreneur aiming to cultivate a sustainable and successful business. By ensuring that you look after your mental well-being, you build a foundation of inner strength that can withstand the pressures and setbacks inherent in network marketing ventures.

Developing a Self-Care Routine

Creating a self-care routine may seem like an indulgence when there are so many business tasks demanding your attention. However, integrating self-care into your daily schedule is a crucial investment in your personal and professional life. This could mean setting aside time for physical activities, engaging in hobbies that relax the mind, or simply ensuring a healthy sleep schedule. It's important to remember that a well-rested and healthy individual is more capable of making sound business decisions and maintaining the energy required to grow a network marketing business.

Establish Boundaries for Work-Life Balance

Work-life balance is critical for mental well-being in the high-stakes environment of network marketing. Establishing clear boundaries between work time and personal time prevents burnout and allows for necessary periods of rest and rejuvenation. For instance, designating specific work hours and adhering to them can give structure to your day and help maintain a sense of normalcy, even as you push toward professional milestones.

Embracing Mindfulness for Emotional Stability

Practicing mindfulness is a powerful way to foster emotional stability. Mindfulness involves being present in the moment and accepting your thoughts without judgment. This practice can greatly reduce stress and anxiety, which are common in any entrepreneurial journey. Whether it's through meditation, deep breathing exercises, or walking in nature, find what works for you to center your mind and reduce the noise of constant business concerns.

Cultivating a Positive Community

Being part of a positive and supportive community is invaluable for sustaining mental well-being. Surround yourself with peers who understand the unique challenges of network marketing and can offer practical advice and emotional support. Additionally, consider seeking out mentors who can guide you through your entrepreneurial journey and provide the wisdom of experience when you encounter obstacles.

Nutrition and Physical Health as a Keystones of Mental Well-being

Never underestimate the correlation between physical health and mental acuity. Proper nutrition, exercise, and regular health check-ups are fundamental to ensuring that your body and mind function optimally. A balanced diet fuels your physical body, while exercise releases endorphins that can improve your mood and reduce stress. Taking care of your physical health is a critical component of remaining mentally sharp and focused on your business objectives.

Conscious Unplugging and Digital Detoxing

In an industry that often emphasizes constant connectivity, learning to consciously unplug can be transformative for your mental health. Periodic digital detoxes can help you break away from the pull of electronic devices and social media, allowing you to reconnect with yourself and your loved ones. This not only helps reduce stress but also refreshes your perspective, enabling you to return to work with a clearer, more innovative mindset.

The Value of Professional Help

There is a significant value in recognizing when professional help is needed. Whether it's consulting a counselor or therapist to navigate through tough times or seeking a coach to help refine your business strategy, reaching out for help is a sign of strength, not weakness. Professional guidance can equip you with tools to manage stress, improve your business acumen, and ultimately enhance your performance in network marketing.

Continuous Learning and Adaptation

In an ever-evolving field like direct sales, it's essential to commit to lifelong learning and adaptation. This includes not only business strategies and market trends but also personal development and mental health awareness. Investing time in learning about stress management techniques, emotional intelligence, and leadership can profoundly impact your resilience and agility in the business world.

Embrace the journey of personal growth alongside your business endeavors. By prioritizing self-care and mental well-being, you'll find that not only is your network marketing business more likely to succeed, but you'll also enjoy the process much more, with a healthy balance that supports lasting fulfillment and success.

Embrace Resilience and Master Your Mindset

In the network marketing industry, **resilience** is not just a desirable trait; it is a prerequisite for success. The ability to bounce back from setbacks, maintain focus amidst challenges, and cultivate a positive attitude are all critical components of a resilient mindset. As you navigate the highs and lows of your network marketing journey, remember that setbacks are not roadblocks but opportunities for growth. **Embrace challenges as steppingstones to your success** and view each obstacle as a chance to sharpen your skills and fortify your determination.

Nurture Your Mental Well-Being

Mindset mastery is the cornerstone of sustained success in network marketing. By implementing techniques to maintain focus and drive, you empower yourself to overcome any obstacle that comes your way.

Practice visualization, affirmations, and goal setting to keep your mindset aligned with your aspirations. Cultivate a growth mindset that embraces challenges as learning opportunities, and celebrate your successes, no matter how small. Remember, your mindset shapes your reality, so **nurture it with positivity and determination**.

Prioritize Self-Care for Entrepreneurial Resilience

Self-care is not a luxury; it is a necessity for entrepreneurial resilience. Just as you nourish your body with healthy food and exercise, you must also prioritize your mental well-being. Take time for activities that recharge your spirit, whether it's meditation, exercise, reading, or spending time with loved ones.

Self-care is not selfish; it is a vital investment in your success. When you prioritize your well-being, you cultivate the inner strength needed to weather any storm that comes your way.

In the fast-paced world of network marketing, **cultivating resilience and mastering your mindset are the keys to long-term success**. By fostering a resilient mindset, implementing mindset mastery techniques, and prioritizing self-care, you lay the foundation for a thriving network marketing business.

Embrace challenges, stay focused on your goals, and take care of your mental well-being. With these practices in place, you are equipped to navigate the ever-changing landscape of the network marketing industry with grace and determination.

Chapter 10: Ascending the Pyramid to Financial Liberation

Julia's fingers dallied over the keyboard, a hesitation borne of that familiar tension between hope and the smoldering embers of disillusionment. The sun, in its afternoon zenith, poured through the window, casting her keys in a warm, golden glow as if to infuse her with its radiance and resolve. Yet, it was a day like any other in the modest office of her suburban home, a sanctuary that witnessed her grapple with the myths and prospects of multi-level marketing (network marketing), this beast that promised riches with the right mastery.

Her mind skimmed over the burgeoning collection of anecdotes, both from newfound mentors and the cautionary tales seemingly baked into the wallpaper of internet forums. They painted a variegated tapestry of success and woe. She would often catch herself, a leaf in the gusting winds of skepticism and credulity, floating from one narrative to the other. Did she dare scale this pyramid, or was she destined to become a mere stone in its base, laden with regrets?

There it was, the scent of jasmine from the garden mingling with the afternoon air, roused by a gentle breeze that stirred her papers. Each one carried the ink of her developing strategies, the embryonic outlines of an action plan personalized as her immutable thumbprint. She had chewed on every word from "Pyramid Ascendants," as if absorbing the chapters could transubstantiate into her very own roadmap. The book was her talisman, well-thumbed, bristling with post-its and hope.

The tinkle of the wind chime interrupted as the neighbor's cat, a sleek, confident creature, made its languorous passage across the fence top. She envied its poise, unburdened by the concerns of financial strategies and personal achievement. Yet, it also served as an unwitting oracle, its grace and freedom emblematic of the life she yearned to capture—a life casting aside the shackles of her nine-to-five.

And so, Julia sat there, a sentinel at the crossroads of decision, colored by the twin hues of fear and ambition. The chair beneath her, a silent companion, seemed to hold its breath along with her. If only the wood and fabric could offer counsel. Could she truly marshal the sagacity and courage to bend the network marketing narrative to her will, to transcend the myths and wield her efforts as the architect of her fate? Would tomorrow find her fortified with newfound conviction or retreating in the face of adversity's snarl?

Sweeping her gaze again over the pages before her, aspirations and strategies whispering in silent symphony, she couldn't help but wonder: Is the ascent of this pyramid a journey of empowerment or merely an illusion dressed in finery of ambition?

The Ultimate Metamorphosis in Multi-level Marketing

Innumerable individuals venture into the world of multi-level marketing with a myriad of misconceptions and misleading apprehensions that often lead to disillusionment. Yet, there lies an untapped reservoir of potential within network marketing that can pave the road to financial liberation and entrepreneurial success. **The pivotal step** in realizing this potential is transforming those pervasive myths into actionable, informed strategies for network marketing prosperity. Insights from industry pioneers, combined with rigorous research, have revealed that a harmonious blend of dedication, strategic planning, and community building is the key to ascend the earning pyramid.

Embarking on this transformative journey requires not just a change in tactics but a revolution in mindset. It is here, at this crossroads of enlightenment and enterprise, that one can synthesize the tools provided in earlier chapters of this very book into a personalized and comprehensive action plan. Each reader's blueprint will be as unique as their ambitions, yet universal principles of direct selling, network building, and product evangelism form the consistent foundation for all to build upon.

The path to network marketing mastery and subsequent financial independence is not shrouded in secrets held by the few but is a testament to the power of duplicable systems and consistent follow-through. **Guided action** is the lodestar that mitigates the risk of stagnation. Readers will learn how to set definitive goals, measure progress, and adjust tactics with agility—all while upholding the highest ethical standards that dignify the industry.

Understanding the essence of multi-level marketing and learning to navigate its intricacies is the cornerstone of this chapter. Here, you will discover how to effectively leverage your personal brand, foster enduring customer relationships, and generate a sustainable income stream. All these are primordial tasks to conquer if one wishes to confidently progress through each level of the network marketing structure, ultimately reaping the rewards of diligent, smart work.

Community building stands at the heart of a successful business. A nurturing, supportive network not only fuels business growth but also fosters a culture of empowerment among its members. Sharing knowledge and celebrating each small victory paves the way for a dynamic and robust salesforce, one that transcends the sum of its parts. This resonance of shared success echoes the overarching themes of mentorship, resilience, and progress that have been meticulously laid out in preceding chapters.

The final chapter before the conclusion reflects the journey thus far and a compass towards the uncharted territories of network marketing achievements that lie ahead. Not merely a capstone, this chapter weaves together the essential threads of knowledge into a cohesive action plan designed for the intrepid entrepreneur. By engaging with these evidential strategies, readers will elevate from fledgling marketers to savvy business operators—the architects of their own financial destinies.

In essence, *Pyramid Ascendants* arms readers with the veritable wisdom needed to launch and grow a thriving multi-level marketing enterprise. Implementing the straightforward, actionable strategies detailed within these pages can set you on a course to financial triumph. For those looking to sustain momentum and hit targets in as little as 12 months, this book serves as your compass—eschewing the common setbacks that befall many and guiding towards a future where your entrepreneurial spirit is not just dreamt about but lived and breathed.

In network marketing there exist numerous myths and misconceptions that often cloud the pathway to success for aspiring entrepreneurs. These barriers can create apprehension and doubt, hindering individuals from fully embracing the opportunities that network marketing presents.

However, by transforming these myths and apprehensions into informed strategies, one can navigate the network marketing landscape with clarity and confidence. It is essential to debunk the myths surrounding network marketing and replace them with practical knowledge and actionable insights to pave the way for success.

One common misconception is that network marketing is a pyramid scheme and inherently fraudulent. Any legitimate network marketing businesses must operate within the bounds of the law, focusing on the sale of products or services to an end consumer. By understanding the difference between pyramid schemes and reputable network marketing companies, individuals can make informed decisions about their participation in this industry. Education and discernment are key to distinguishing between legitimate network marketing opportunities and fraudulent schemes.

Another prevalent myth is that success in network marketing is reserved for a select few with specific skills or backgrounds. This belief can deter individuals from pursuing their entrepreneurial ambitions within the network marketing space. In truth, success in network marketing is attainable for anyone willing to put in the effort, learn the necessary skills, and adapt to the dynamic nature of the industry. **With dedication and a willingness to learn, individuals from diverse backgrounds can thrive in the world of network marketing.**

Moreover, the misconception that network marketing requires significant upfront investment without guarantee of returns can instill fear in potential entrepreneurs. While starting a network marketing business may involve some initial costs, it is important to approach investments strategically and cautiously. **By conducting thorough research, setting realistic goals, and leveraging available resources, individuals can mitigate financial risks and maximize their chances of success in network marketing.**

A crucial strategy for dispelling myths and overcoming apprehensions in network marketing is to seek mentorship and guidance from experienced individuals in the field. **Mentors can provide valuable insights, share their experiences, and offer support and encouragement to those navigating the complexities of network marketing.** Building a strong support network within the network marketing community can foster growth, learning, and collaboration, enabling individuals to overcome challenges and achieve their entrepreneurial goals.

Continue reading to discover how to transform myths into steppingstones towards network marketing success.

After grasping the foundational concepts and insights outlined in the previous sections, it's time to distill this knowledge into a personalized action plan that will pave your way to success in the network marketing arena. **Synthesizing the strategies and tools offered in this guide is the key to crafting a roadmap tailored to your strengths, goals, and aspirations.**

Begin by revisiting your understanding of the myths surrounding network marketing and how to dispel them with practical truths. By internalizing these realities, you can build a solid foundation for your network marketing journey.

Reflect on your unique strengths, skills, and interests to determine how they align with the opportunities presented in the network marketing landscape. Consider how leveraging your strengths can propel you forward in your entrepreneurial pursuits.

Craft a clear vision of where you want to be in your network marketing business in the next six months, one year and beyond. Visualizing your success can help you stay focused and motivated during challenging times.

Set specific, measurable, achievable, relevant, and time-bound (SMART) goals that will guide your actions and measure your progress. Break down these goals into actionable steps that you can take daily, weekly, and monthly to move closer to your desired outcomes. **Consistency and dedication** in implementing these actions are key to building momentum and achieving sustainable growth in your network marketing business.

Establish a support system of like-minded individuals, mentors, or accountability partners who can provide guidance, motivation, and feedback along your network marketing journey.

Surrounding yourself with a positive and empowering network can fuel your ambition and keep you accountable to your goals. **Continuously evaluate your progress**, assess what is working well, and be willing to adapt and pivot in response to challenges or changing circumstances.

Invest in your personal development by seeking out training, resources, and opportunities for growth within the network marketing industry. Stay informed about market trends, best practices, and innovations that can enhance your business acumen and effectiveness as an entrepreneur.

Embrace a mindset of continuous learning and improvement to stay ahead of the curve in the competitive network marketing landscape.

Celebrate your achievements, no matter how small, and use them as milestones to inspire further progress. Recognize the effort and dedication you put into your network marketing business and acknowledge the positive impact it has on your financial well-being and personal growth.

Stay committed to your action plan, remain resilient in the face of setbacks, and stay focused on your long-term vision of financial liberation through network marketing mastery.

By translating insights into actionable steps, you can chart a course towards network marketing success with clarity and purpose. Your personalized action plan will serve as a compass, guiding you through challenges and opportunities as you ascend the network marketing pyramid towards your goals of financial independence and entrepreneurial fulfillment. Trust in your abilities, stay true to your vision, and take decisive steps towards realizing your ambitions in the dynamic world of network marketing.

The First Step: Self-Evaluation and Commitment

Embarking on the path to network marketing mastery and financial independence starts with a critical self-evaluation. Assess your strengths, weaknesses, and personal goals. **Ask yourself what you hope to achieve** through network marketing - be it financial freedom, personal development, or the ability to work independently. Acknowledge that this endeavor requires a commitment much like any other business pursuit - it demands time, effort, and a mindset geared towards continuous learning. Your commitment is the foundation upon which your network marketing success will be built. Remember, this is not a 'get rich quick' scheme; it's a systematic approach to building a sustainable income stream over time.

Understanding the Market and Products

Gain in-depth knowledge of the network marketing market and the products you will be promoting. This is not just about knowing the features and benefits but understanding the actual value they offer to customers. *Align your products with the needs* and desires of your target market. Cultivate an expertise in your niche that allows you to converse with authority and confidence. The better you understand your offerings, the more effectively you can communicate their importance and build trust with prospective clients and team members.

Building Relationships

In network marketing, success is largely dependent on the relationships you build. Networking is at the core of this business model; it's about connecting with people on a genuine level. *Approach each interaction with sincerity* and a desire to add value to the other person's life. Whether it's through solving a problem, addressing a need, or simply listening, your relationships can determine the longevity and prosperity of your network marketing career. Cultivating trust and loyalty will create a foundation for a robust and supportive network.

Structured Goal Setting

Clear and structured goal setting is fundamental. Establish short-term and long-term goals, breaking them down into actionable tasks. This segmentation will help you stay focused and measure your progress. Keep your objectives SMART - Specific, Measurable, Achievable, Relevant, and Time-bound. Boldly set targets that challenge you yet are within reach with persistent effort. Regularly revising and updating your goals will keep you aligned with the dynamic nature of the network marketing market.

Leveraging Systems and Tools

Optimize your workflow by leveraging available systems and tools designed for network marketing businesses. Tools for customer relationship management (CRM), communication, and organization can drastically increase your productivity and efficiency.

Utilize training resources provided by your network marketing company and seek out additional educational materials to enhance your skill set. Embrace the technology and methodologies that can streamline your operations, freeing up time to concentrate on growth.

Personal Branding

Your personal brand is a powerful asset in the network marketing industry. It distinguishes you from the competition and can attract the right clients and team members. Show the unique value you bring to the table - be it through your exceptional service, insights, or leadership qualities. Cultivate an online presence that resonates with your core values and professional ethos. *Authentically represent yourself*, and your personal brand will become a magnet for success.

Consistency and Adaptability

Consistency in your efforts is what compounds over time to yield results. But equally important is adaptability—the ability to respond to changes in the market, within your network marketing company, or in consumer behaviors. Stay informed and be prepared to pivot strategies as necessary. *Never underestimate the power of persistence* coupled with the willingness to evolve; it's a combination that many successful network marketing entrepreneurs attribute their success to.

Community and Giving Back

In network marketing, it is just as much about giving back as it is about achieving personal success. Participating in community events, mentoring others, and contributing to collective growth helps foster an environment of mutual success.

Empower others on their journey and find ways to contribute to societal well-being. This approach not only enriches your network but also builds an enduring, positive reputation that transcends mere financial outcomes.

The Pursuit of Growth

Never stop learning and growing. The realm of network marketing is continuously evolving, and staying on top of trends, techniques, and self-improvement is crucial. Prioritize personal development and professional training as core aspects of your routine. Seek out mentors, attend seminars, and consume relevant content. The pursuit of growth will keep you agile, informed, and ready to seize new opportunities as they arise.

With the right strategies and a steadfast commitment to your entrepreneurial journey, you have the blueprint to advance through the ranks of network marketing and achieve the financial liberation you desire. The pathway is set before you, and each step you take is one closer to your ultimate goal of financial independence and personal life fulfillment.

Final Thoughts

As we wrap up our journey towards mastering network marketing and achieving financial liberation, it's crucial to reflect on the core themes and lessons that have guided us thus far. By dispelling myths, embracing informed strategies, and crafting personalized action plans, we have laid a solid foundation for success in the multi-level marketing realm.

Transforming apprehensions into strategies empowers us to navigate the network marketing landscape with clarity and purpose. By challenging misconceptions and embracing proven techniques, we unlock the potential for exponential growth and sustainable success. Each myth overcome becomes a steppingstone towards our entrepreneurial goals.

Synthesizing insights into personalized action plans is where the blueprint for success truly takes shape. By leveraging the tools and guidance provided, we can tailor our approach to fit our unique strengths and aspirations. With a clear roadmap in hand, we are equipped to navigate obstacles, seize opportunities, and drive our network marketing business towards prosperity.

Embarking on a guided journey towards network marketing

mastery is the culmination of our efforts. With determination, perseverance, and a commitment to continuous improvement, we set ourselves on a path towards financial independence and personal fulfillment. Each step taken brings us closer to realizing our entrepreneurial dreams and unlocking the full potential of our network marketing endeavors.

As you venture forth, remember that the power to transform your financial future lies within your hands. By harnessing the lessons learned, embracing challenges as opportunities for growth, and staying true to your vision, you will ascend the network marketing pyramid towards a brighter, more prosperous tomorrow. Your journey towards financial freedom begins now. **Embrace it with determination, focus, and unwavering belief in your ability to succeed.**

A Journey Towards Unleashing Your Entrepreneurial Potential

As we draw the curtains on this journey together, it's important to reflect on the road we've traversed, the myths we've debunked, and the strategies we've forged to pave a path towards mastering the art of multi-level marketing. The blueprint laid out within these pages is more than just a guide; it's a testament to the belief in the power of transformation through perseverance, knowledge, and strategic action.

Real-world applications of this content are vast and varied. Whether you're just starting out or you're looking to refine your network marketing approach, the principles outlined here are designed to be your compass - guiding you through challenges, helping you leverage opportunities, and equipping you to achieve sustainable success. The journey of entrepreneurship is one of constant learning, adjustment, and growth. With the insights garnered from this book, you're better prepared to navigate this journey, armed with a deeper understanding of how to harness your unique strengths and the dynamics of network marketing to your advantage.

Recapitulating the core essence of our discussion, we started by addressing the skepticism surrounding network marketing, dissecting the myths, and laying bare the facts. We journeyed through understanding the human mind's immense power in shaping our reality, drawing from my deep-seated belief in and knowledge about the cultivation of human potential. With a mix of carefully curated case studies, proven strategies, and personal anecdotes, the book aimed to provide a solid foundation for building a prosperous network marketing business while steering clear of common pitfalls.

Putting these learnings into action involves several clear steps. Begin by setting concrete, achievable goals, both short-term and long-term, based on the realistic assessment of your current position and where you wish to be.

Cultivate a network of mentors and peers who share your aspirations and values, as their support and guidance will be invaluable as you progress. Additionally, consistently apply the marketing strategies and leadership principles discussed, while staying adaptable to the ever-evolving landscape of the network marketing industry.

While the content of this book is comprehensive, I acknowledge that the network marketing landscape is dynamic, with new challenges and opportunities constantly emerging. Continuous learning and adaptation are not just recommended; they're necessary for long-term success. In this light, I encourage further research and exploration into the areas we've discussed, and beyond, to keep pace with the industry's growth and your personal development as an entrepreneur.

The power to change your future, to turn dreams into tangible realities, rests within you. Embrace the journey with an open heart and an eager mind, committed to personal growth and the betterment of those around you. By doing so, you not only pave the way for your own success but also contribute positively to the community, reinforcing the belief that true success encompasses both personal achievements and the upliftment of others.

In closing, let the words of Henry Ford resonate with you as you embark on or continue your entrepreneurial voyage:

"Whether you think you can, or you think you can't—you're right."

These words encapsulate the essence of our discourse on mindset, potential, and the power of belief in shaping our destiny. Armed with the knowledge, strategies, and insights from this book, the path to network marketing mastery and entrepreneurial success lies open before you. It's your journey to take, your dream to realize.

Remember, the journey of a thousand miles begins with a single step. Take that step today, with confidence and conviction, toward realizing your entrepreneurial spirit and unlocking the doors to financial freedom and a life of abundance.

Best wishes for tremendous Success!

Dustin Cohen

JOIN OUR SUCCESS COMMUNITY FOR BUSINESS TIPS

NeTWORK MARKeTING
LIFESTYLES

NETWORKMARKETINGLIFESTYLES.COM

Network Marketing Lifestyles is the Industries Premiere Website

Read in depth articles about top companies, success stories, industry news, trends, social media marketing, legal issues, success tips, motivation, and much more. This is a top-notch online community rivaling the quality and content of other every other industry website such as: MLM GATEWAY, BUSINESS FROM HOME, WORLD OF DIRECT SELLING, DIRECT SELLING NEWS, SOCIAL SELLING NEWS, MLM NATION, MLM LEGAL, WARRIOR FORUM, and NETWORK MARKETING MAGAZINE.

Made in the USA
Coppell, TX
10 April 2024

31122999R10079